IMPROVE YOUR SOCIAL SKILLS

IMPROVE YOUR SOCIAL SKILLS

ADAM NIGHT

TABLE OF CONTENTS

INTRODUCTION

This is not the usual useless book that tells you so many words of encouragement. It is not a self help book. And it is not a fictionalized content about how good it is to make friends. If you plan to find comfort in this book, you can throw it away right now. If you need someone to console you, tell you "poor boy / girl, all alone and no one wants to make friends with him / her", then do something immediately: go in front of the mirror and slap yourself. Stop compliments, stop useless words.

Now it's time to change and we'll do it together.

Do you feel lonely? Do you look around and see that all people seem bright and intelligent when they talk? Do you always think too much about the words you have to say when you want to impress someone? Even when you have to buy bread, do you always need to think carefully about what you have to say?

Well, you know exactly what your problem is and in this book you can find the solution.

The critical point in any problematic solution is to understand that you have a problem. And this is extremely logical and to make you understand I want to tell you the story of Andrew Slown and the biggest mistake of his life.

Andrew works in a large car retail company and plays an important role in the administration department. He is a quiet person, very polite and who loves to give his best every day.

All his colleagues think he is an extremely quiet person, but in reality Andrew's head is always filled with a huge amount of words. But Andrew can't always say everything he thinks. Every morning Andrew goes to a bar in front of his workplace and has breakfast. Macchiato coffee and croissant with apricot jam. Every day for seven years.

But do you know something that nobody knows except Andrew?

He hates milk in coffee and above all hates jam-filled croissants.

Yes exactly, Andrew hates these two things but every morning he goes to his usual bar and orders with his smile the usual croissant stuffed with jam and a coffee with a little milk. Every single day.

Now I want to tell you why. On the first day of work, Andrew was extremely tense and excited about the new life project he was about to undertake. After a degree in Economics, full marks and compliments from his university professors, Andrew was about to start something really important. A serious job. A real job. He didn't have to deliver pizzas like he did when he was sixteen for ten dollars and a pizza with mushrooms. He didn't even have to try to teach the Pythagorean theorem to a younger student in those tough hours of private lessons.

Andrew Slown got up early that morning and needed breakfast. He saw a bar, it was nice and looked very clean so he decided to come in and ask for coffee. The young girl at the bar smiled at him and asked "macchiato?".

Sixty seconds of embarrassment and anxiety. In Andrew's mind there was emptiness but also a cascade of words and doubts. Andrew feared that it might be rude to answer with a very normal "no, thank you". And that smile rang in his head. Within a few seconds, a myriad of reasons appeared and disappeared. Lactose intolerance, intestinal indisposition, momentary desire for black coffee, desire for a stronger coffee to wake up well - you know, yesterday I went to bed late I went out with friends I'm a cool guy. Or a simple no, thanks I don't like it.

Andrew couldn't say any of this and a simple "yes, thank you" came out of his mouth. And then a stupid smile. "And a croissant, please."

"Yes, the one with the jam is fine. Perfect. Really, I love jam."

This moment marked the following seven years in Andrew's life and also represents the biggest mistake in his life.

Perhaps it may seem silly but I invite you to think seriously about all that this has involved in your life.

From that day on, Andrew felt involved with the staff in that bar and could not go to another bar.

Every morning Andrew starts the day with a coffee and a croissant he hates.

Stained coffee does not have the same effect as black coffee on Andrew and therefore as soon as it arrives in the office you take another coffee from the automatic machine.

Every morning Andrew offers coffee to two of his colleagues at the vending machine, they in turn offer Andrew a coffee at half past ten and at noon. The result is an excessive level of caffeine which makes him even more tense.

Andrew looks at the croissants filled with chocolate cream every morning, looks at them with desire but never takes them because he can't say it. The result is that every morning he goes to the office with this desire and feels frustrated.

All these things may seem silly. But the real problem is Andrew is sick and does not understand what his problem is. His excessive level of shyness does not allow him to say what he thinks and to express himself freely. Andrew is an adult, he is a willing worker and a good person. But he can't say what he thinks.

This is a serious problem. Andrew has a lack of social skills and doesn't know it.

Here this is the turning point in the life of every person: understanding which problems exist in one's life, being aware of why things are not going as one would like.

Awareness: this is the first big step towards a better life and in this book I will explain you how to reach it and how to start from it to get everything you want.

There are so many people who hold back and fail to express their feelings: a real army of detainees: we can thus define all those myriads of people who are unable to express their opposition and who therefore live with a world of emotions and thoughts that cannot unfold.

There are those who always say yes and even seem enthusiastic about the choices of others, so as not to show their disappointment, and those who lower their eyes hoping that the interlocutor miraculously intuit his state of mind; there are those who set up a timid discourse but take it so far away that it never goes to the point, and those who remain dumbfounded by giving the idea of "those who keep silent". But in all cases the frustration of not being able to resist grows more and more, polluting life.

The problem is often contained in the fear of others' judgment and in the idea of not being accepted. The logical consequence is a splitting of the behavior, which becomes almost a split of the personality: on the one hand the detainees manifest "everything and more", that is they do not just say everything they think, but they overturn the whole load of frustrations, of anger and problems arising from relations with the world, so that this relationship risks collapse; on the other, with all the others, they live in a state of adaptation, without anyone noticing, except when, occasionally, they fall into an explosion of crying or a hysterical scene. But at that point the expression of discomfort is so altered and excessive, that it is considered as an oddity and, punctually, misjudged. And this is exactly what you wanted to avoid.

Here it is. If you think you are one of these people, I want to give you the first advice to finally be free and happy. Go to the bathroom and wash your face. Use plenty of fresh water. A lot.

You have done? Well. Now look in the mirror and look at your face well. Answer the questions that follow with sincerity.

1. Did this behavior lead me to be happy and satisfied?
2. Did I get to feel accepted in relationships?
3. Did this attitude make me have authentic and spontaneous relationships?

We all know that the answer will always be the same: no.

You have created a precarious balance in your life, in which your true nature, part of some fortunate circumstance, cannot come out. From this awareness comes a second great truth about your life. You need to get out of egocentrism. The detainee lives as always cut off from the choices that count, as a "predestined victim": on the one hand there is him, who is not understood because he cannot make himself understood, on the other there is the whole world, which is not he can understand his inner drama and does nothing to soothe it, on the contrary, he often takes advantage of it. It may seem strange, but this is exactly how it is, paradoxically, always seeing oneself far from the center is a convoluted way to put oneself in the center. It is a twisted ego-centrism.

What you have to do? You have to get back into the game.

The best thing you can do is give up, shout to yourself that you never want to have this negative, defensive, not spectacular egocentrism, but still egocentrism.

This book is the result of a great research activity and of personal experiences deepened and observed according to specific techniques of self-knowledge. Precisely because of this great work that has been done, I invite you at the end of reading the book to leave a positive review on Amazon.

So let's start, my dear friend. The time has come to get rid of everything that does not allow you to feel good with others and therefore with yourself.

ALL MEN ARE ISLANDS

A poem famous all over the world said that *No man is an island.* This is a beautiful concept. A declaration of love towards the human race. We are not alone. We are all surrounded by people to discover and interact with. It's all very nice, really.

Yet the truth is another. The truth is that we are all single people living in a world that is sometimes difficult to deal with. It is not easy to feel at ease and often we prefer to close ourselves in silence and in states of solitude. Being alone is reassuring, being alone is something that allows you not to have to think too much about what to say. You don't need to be polite, you don't need to look smart, you can laugh at things that are too stupid, you can go around the house wearing only your underwear.

The life of each of us can be invaded by a profound sense of solitude. It is the condemnation of the modern man but it is also an important starting point to understand that your social difficulties are not a wall too high to climb. You can defeat your loneliness, you can do it and you can start today if you want.

So the right question is: do you want to defeat your loneliness?

See this blank line up here? Take a pen and write the answer to the question I asked you. Attention, not a pencil. Take an indelible pen and write the answer. This is the true beginning of a better life.

And if you don't have a pen and can't write your answer, then stop and close the book. Find a pen, find it, bring it here now. Then write the answer and then continue to read this book.

There are moments in life when even when you are surrounded by people you feel a deep sense of inner loneliness.

You still carry out your routine activities but feel that feeling of emptiness in your chest, or a big boulder in your stomach. It is the sense of loneliness and you perceive it clearly when you feel disconnected from life, from yourself and from the people around you.

How to overcome loneliness when it seems so deeply rooted inside?

Although at this moment it seems to you that few things make sense and you are pervaded by a sense of desperation and sadness, you can heal it, alleviate it and step by step back to live fully and to the fullest of your joy.

THE THREE STEPS OF SUCCESS

Now I want to tell you something important. Or rather, I want to ask you something important: can you count up to three?

I really hope so. Because now I'm about to reveal the three secret steps to success in this fight against loneliness. These are three essential steps. So sit back, relax and read these three points well. When you are done, think about your life. Re-read them again and find examples of how to apply these concepts to your daily life.

STEP # 1 GRAB YOUR AWARENESS

Don't ignore it. Choose to bring maximum awareness to what you are experiencing. Living by understanding where you are going is fundamental. Do you like that pair of shoes? Great, then buy them. Do you like playing golf? Then you really should start doing it.

You always have to think that in this chaos of things that happen every day the real important thing is the feeling that you experience every day while you live and do things. Think about how your body feels, the emptiness you feel in your chest and the tension in your throat, listen to that boulder that makes your body heavy and tight.

You must listen to your sense of loneliness, do not let sadness escape without understanding what it is and why you are feeling it.

When you allow sadness to be heard, you have just taken the first step to release it and let it go.

STEP #2 THINK OF TODAY AND ACCEPT YOURSELF

Don't run away. Instinctively many people are led to fill moments of emptiness and loneliness with whatever distracts them. Maybe you sleep more than necessary, you frantically try to start new relationships, take refuge on television and watch TV series all the time, movies and movies, or maybe you find yourself facing superficial activities with little meaning.

Of course all these things may even seem interesting and will keep you busy and seem somewhat connected to life. Who doesn't like to watch TV series lying on the bed? The problem is that if your life is made up of only this then you really have a serious lack of something. You miss everything else.

But none of these things really work, at least not profoundly, let alone in the long run. You will feel the loneliness returning in moments of emptiness, perhaps before sleeping and in free time from other activities.

Choose to live this emotion and remember that as an emotion, it will pass. It cannot be otherwise. Meanwhile dedicated to activities and people really significant for you, finding your balance.

Another way in which many face the feeling of loneliness is to blame themselves incessantly for their mistakes, for the things they could have done differently and for those who did wrong.

This is because you hope that by identifying what is wrong with you, you can correct it and then the pain will go away. Or at least you can give a rational sense to all this. In most cases this makes things worse because it leads you to enter an endless circle of self-criticism and negative thoughts.

I want to tell you something important now. Take it easy. Stand up, look at your hands, feel your breath. Feel the passing of time. Count up to twenty loudly. You can analyze why and how for later, now it's not important.

Experience the emotion and find your balance between feeling and reacting.

STEP # 3 SHARE, HEAL AND GET BETTER

Do you go to work in the car? Do you go to school by bus? As soon as you walk out the door there are so many people around you. All these people live in your own world every day and walking the streets see your own things. Yes, your life is unique in the world and you certainly don't have the same problems as that girl who works in the car insurance office and probably the guy who works in the hairdresser in the street behind your house every day faces very different problems from yours. The lawyer who took care of the case against the neighboring building in the morning suffers from heavy breath and the fishmonger hates having sweaty hands all day because of the gloves he has to wear according to the law.

Your aunt gets up every day and can't get perfect hair like her colleague in the office. Your neighbor poured red wine on a carpet that had paid nine hundred euros. Your ex-girlfriend just threw the phone against the wall because she was fired. Your brother hasn't been selected for that stage he cared for. Your old middle school professor has lost his car keys.

Remind yourself that you are not the only one having problems every day and above all you are not the only one feeling alone in times of difficulty.

Feeling lonely is part of the human experience, it is part of life and almost all of us experience this feeling from time to time.

What would you say to a friend of yours who feels this way? Would you hug him or blame him? Would you ask him words of comfort or criticism?

Treat yourself as you would treat your best friend. Be compassionate. Look at yourself in perspective, without judging or condemning yourself and take care of yourself in small everyday gestures. Find comfort and support in the loved ones you have in your life. Take a deep breath, take the phone and tell them how you feel, ask for help in the form you need most. Sometimes a word, a hug and a couple of small words can suffice.

Have you read these three fundamental steps towards success?

Well. Now re-read everything and then move on to these Three Practical Exercises. You must do it. If you don't want to do it think that by now you are at stake, you are reading this book and you have agreed to do everything in your power to improve your life. These three exercises are part of the strategies to finally be free to express yourself and to eliminate loneliness from your everyday life.

Practical exercise n.1 - Unconscious muscles.

Do you know that the human body has so many muscles that you don't even know you have? They are called unconscious muscles. They have always been there since you were born but you didn't even know you had them and above all you don't know how to exploit them. Now go to the wall and stand in profile resting the outer side of it. Push with all the strength you have towards the outside. Think you had to raise your arm and use all the strength you have in your arm to lift it even if the wall stops you. Push again, push. Hold your arm in this way for two minutes. Then move away from the wall and give space to the arm. What's going on? The arm rises by itself. You didn't tell him to get up but his arm is rising. This is an unconscious muscle that is making you raise your arm and now you are aware of having it. Likewise, you need to be aware of who you are and the problems you face every day.

Practical exercise n.2 - The word of the sea

Do you have any beaches near your place? Go there. If there are no beaches, look for a place where there is no one. The ideal would be to find a place you like, a place where you feel at ease and of which you love the setting. Go there and watch everything around you. Open air. The wind blows? Is it hot or cold? Are there clouds in the sky? There are so many trees. Look carefully at everything in front of you and describe it aloud. Do not laugh. Speak slowly and list everything you see out loud and safe. Remember that you are saying all true things and you must be sure of yourself. Trust yourself. When you finish listing what you see, think about your life. Do you feel lonely? What is your relationship with others? Are you satisfied with what you have? Answer aloud and deal with your answers. Repeat them three times. Now you can accept your feelings and your emotions, expose your problems loudly and accept the situation. This will be the best starting point for your new happy life.

Practical Exercise # 3 - Help the neighbor

There is a theory that if every person in the world helped seven people close, then the world would be better in just one month. In fact, a chain of mutual aid and social well-being would be formed that anyone could benefit from. And here is your practical exercise. Take a pen and paper and write the names of seven people you see often, they don't have to be people you are in confidence with. They can also be simple strangers. Maybe people you see every day on the street. Choose seven people and find seven ways to improve their lives.

THE RULE OF NUTS ON THE TABLE

When I visit my grandmother, she always brings me a bowl of peanuts. When I go with my friends to the bar for a beer, we need a small bowl of peanuts and chips on the table. Every second Tuesday of the month, my mother comes home and brings me fresh vegetables she buys at the market. We sit down, take two glasses of orange juice and a bowl of peanuts so we eat and drink while we chat about how to cook zucchini with sage and garlic.

A bowl of peanuts is something extremely simple. Peanuts can be served in small or large bowls, with or without a teaspoon to serve, in small single portion containers. Peanuts are something extremely familiar and conversational. They are not at all like the chips or any other fancy little food to eat while drinking something and chatting amiably.

Peanuts are something to share and eat little by little. Slowly. Then quickly. They seem to never end because if you eat peanuts too quickly they don't taste the same.

Now I want us to take the mental image of the peanuts and apply them to everyday life and efforts to overcome the difficulties encountered when trying to make friends and fail.

Why the peanuts?

Simple: I chose peanuts because they represent exactly what we want to achieve.

1. Sharing
2. Long lasting relationships
3. Emotions at each peanut
4. Happy moments

So here is the time to reveal the Rule of the Bowl of Peanuts.

When you find yourself in situations where you do not feel comfortable such as:

- parties and social events with people you don't know
- work meetings with colleagues and professionals from other companies
- dialogues with customers
- speeches in front of a teacher or your boss
- vacation with friends or strangers
- discussions with neighbors
- meetings with close relatives and distant members of your family

focus a bowl of peanuts on the table. Summon with your mind the comfortable situation and the extremely pleasant and social atmosphere you have when you are sitting at a table with peanuts to share.

It is an important emotion, to be taken seriously. Feel the pleasure of having a bowl of peanuts to share and live the moment following this secret rule.

"The new relationships must be addressed as we face a bowl of peanuts: calmly, lightly, chatting without commitment with people for as long as sharing the peanuts lasts."

HOW TO MAKE FRIENDS EVERY DAY, OVERCOMING YOUR SOCIAL PROBLEMS

In ancient times survival depended on the people you had around you. Living in groups allowed them to better defend themselves from predators and hunt animals for food. So he allowed you to take the hide away.

But today, what are the advantages of having friends? You can live well even while being quiet and isolated with my PC at home. Today you don't have to defend yourself from lions or hunt a bunch of buffalo to feed you.

Why should you create and cultivate quality friendships?

Simple. Scientific studies report how having quality friendships can greatly improve your life, your health and your mood.

For a full and fulfilling life, having good friends is an indispensable condition.

Making new friends should be a simple task, but unfortunately it is often not that easy job we all think. Since in many cases making friends requires leaving your comfort zone, creating new ties with new people can be difficult. Among these, for example, shyness, fear of dislike etc.

Fortunately, to make friends it is not necessary to be "socialists" and to be immersed for 24 hours a week in chats, parties and aperitifs. Even if you are introverted you will be able to do very well by putting into practice the advice that will follow.

Finding new friends is an activity that never ends in life. It is inevitable that the people with whom we are friends face events that over time distance them from us, like getting married, developing new passions or you may simply want to close an old friendship that "no longer works".

This is why knowing how to make friends remains an important skill for life and not just during childhood and adolescence.

I need all your attention now. It is really important because I am going to make you think about some essential steps that will reveal how to make friends and how to overcome your social problems.

These steps must be considered in terms of these six precious universal principles of friendship:

1) **sincerely be interested in others**
2) **smile**
3) **call people by name**
4) **encourage them to talk about themselves and listen to them**
5) **talk about what interests others**
6) **make them feel important**

STEP 1. WHERE TO MEET FRIENDS?

According to the theory of proximity (proximity theory) we become friends with people who live geographically close to us or who frequent the places where we usually go. So the first step is to leave the house. Here are some areas where you can typically make new knowledge.

– Workplace: make friends with colleagues.

- People you already know: such as relatives, neighbors, friends of friends.
- Birthdays are an excellent opportunity to meet friends
- Animal friends. Associations for animal friends and animal defenders.
- Professional events. Professional events (such as courses, seminars, workshops) are a great way to meet people you already know have a common interest with you.

The idea is to seize the opportunities that arise spontaneously and without being, at least at the beginning, too wary or selective. On the selection process I will speak better at the end of the book.

STEP 2. THE TECHNIQUE "TELL ME MORE"

This technique works very well and is really simple. Combined with good body language and effective active listening it can be a great way to make contact with another person.

The technique serves to show a sincere interest, in fact many people love to talk about themselves and feel important if someone listens to them and asks them questions. This is also a great way to find out if you have interests in common and if you find something in common, it could also become a good excuse to get to know you better and do something together.

To show interest there are some "magic" phrases that lead to continue the conversation in a natural way: "really?", "Ah yes?", "Interesting ..." Another way to show interest is to raise the eyebrows and smile. Raising eyebrows is in fact a non-verbal signal which means I'm listening to you and paying attention to you. It's like saying I'm interested, I want to know everything you have to say without really saying it.

Happy little note: smile, smile and smile again.

That's right! Laughter is good for health and is an excellent social glue. It is important to create a positive and pleasant first experience that you can both remember with a smile. The ideal situation will be reached when you both return home thinking "I was fine, I want to see him again". This obviously does not mean having to be pressured to make the experience overly enjoyable, remember that it is important that you are first and foremost yourself. Suggest a venue that will allow you to talk. Avoid the rooms with deafening music and choose one instead with some form of entertainment that gives you the possibility of not having to talk all the time. This is important because it will allow you to get to know yourself better without pressure to continue the conversation continuously.

FOCUS ON THINGS THAT BOTH OF YOU MIGHT LIKE

Another element to make people want to see you again is to use positive emotions. The more positive your attitude will be, the more you will tend to be attractive. So remember not to take yourself too seriously and relax.

According to the effect of "mere exposure" seeing a person several times makes us like it more (principle of familiarity); for this reason it is important to make sure that the potential friend wants to see us again.

The ideal way to start putting into practice the three-step approach is through a simple commitment like this. Take a blank sheet of paper and write this sentence:

**"To meet new people here is what I will do every week:
_____ "**

See the blank space line? Fill it with sincerity and commitment. Then attach the sheet on the bathroom mirror of your home and respect your intentions.

Friendship is more than an option in life. It is an indispensable feeling in the formation of an individual who goes through all the phases of life. For this reason, knowing how to cultivate and create quality friendships is an extremely valuable skill that remains valid over time.

Now calm down, sit down and relax. You have just read something really important and you have to have time to metabolize all these principles. So close the book, you'll continue to read later. Now put your shoes on and go out for a walk, breathe the air outside and put into practice all the valuable advice you just read.

THE TONES OF YOUR VOIC

W hat basic tool do you have at your disposal to make friends and relate to other people around you?

THE VOICE

The voice is something extremely powerful and that many people unfortunately underestimate.

The importance of the voice is given precisely by its metacommunicative function: it manifests and induces emotions in the interlocutor, it can arouse empathy, detachment, attention, distraction, trust, agitation.

The paraverbale language indicates the set of sounds emitted in the communication and the importance of the voice is given by different aspects:

The tone, which is influenced by physiological factors (age, physical constitution) and by the context: for example a person of high social level who finds himself speaking with a lower social level will tend to have a more serious tone of voice;

The frequency, and also in this case the social aspect has a strong influence: a person who is talking to a superior will tend to have a wer voice frequency than normal;

Rhythm, which gives greater or lesser authority to the words spoken. Speaking at a slow pace for example, inserting pauses between sentences and perhaps even slightly lowering the volume of the voice, gives a tone of solemnity to what is said with respect to using a higher rhythm. In the analysis of rhythm in the paraverbale language the importance of pauses should also be considered.

Silence is also part of the paraverbale language and its characteristics can often be strongly ambivalent and social and hierarchical aspects play a fundamental role with it.

Very often we talk about what to do in certain situations, but we don't always highlight the mistakes and things not to do. This negative part of the speech is simply very important because it helps you think about what you should avoid doing and the wrong things you do every day.

What are the main errors that are committed underestimating the importance of the voice in the communicative act?

First of all, usually the volume of voice is constantly low or constantly too high, other errors that make communication absolutely non-persuasive are the excessively fast speech, the lack of tonal intensity, the frequent presence of interlayers, the misuse of breaks.

As we have said, the importance of the voice lies in the fact of transmitting emotions, and only after contents, this is why the effective use of the voice includes dynamism. The voice should never be static and fossilized on the same tone trends, but should take on a variable tone, that is, that uses all three types of tones - low, medium, high - in a non-repetitive and unpredictable sequence. In this way the interventions will be more modulated and the interlocutor, or the interlocutors, in the face of changes in tone will certainly maintain a higher level of attention and involvement.

Using the voice dynamically also means using pauses correctly: speaking without stopping always creates in the other a lowering of concentration, furthermore strategic pauses can also be used, together with low and slow tones, to emphasize a word or a sentence within the speech.

Warm, enveloping, or authoritarian, aggressive, low or persuasive, the voice changes according to the person's emotions and character, to his state of health and vitality. But the right volume, tone and timbre, accompanied by a positive attitude, transmit wellbeing to oneself and to others. Let's see how to learn to control and improve one's voice.

We all know that the voice is conditioned by emotions, but few know that the opposite also happens and that emotions can be created, or modified and controlled thanks to the voice. By working on this extraordinary instrument, being aware of its power and then refining it, you can really improve the quality of your life and that of those who listen to us.

Experts classify the item by color:

- yellow, when it is cheerful, nice
- blue, if it is authoritative
- red, in moments of passion
- black, if there is anger and aggression
- gray, when it is apathetic
- green, when it is persuasive and relaxed.

It is precisely this last type of voice that requires concentration to give well-being.

If you want to understand how to use your voice to improve your social skills, first you need to be aware of your voice.

Have you ever heard your voice? Do you know the most important tool at your disposal?

First you need to become familiar with your own tones, tones and voice color.

Practical exercise to do: listen to your own recorded voice. Perhaps you don't know that 98% of people say they don't recognize it and find it unpleasant. There is a big difference between what we think we convey and what we really communicate. Only in situations of anger or extreme sadness do we transmit something more, and this should teach us that behind our words there should always be emotions, and the more positive these are, the easier it will be to communicate sympathy and serenity that in turn predispose who listens to us give positive answers.

THE VOICE OF GREEN COLOR

Adopt a medium-low volume, lower the tone of a tone making it persuasive, confidential, mark the words and pronounce them slowly, take breaks from time to time as if waiting for an answer, for an intervention by the other, to color one's own voice with a cheerful and happy note. In this way a green voice will be obtained, that of trust, constructive relationship and sharing.

A voice like this can have a natural gift, but it can also be learned over time; it should be used as much as possible, in the family and at work, even when someone has been rude or is taking advantage of our patience. The benefits are primarily personal because it gives well-being and relaxation, but it is pleasant to discover the effect this item has on others: empathy, attention, the climate of collaboration.

WHAT TO DO TO MASTER IT? PRACTICE, PRACTICE AND PRACTICE AGAIN.

To learn or strengthen the green tone you need 3 weeks of work for 5 minutes a day; then you will need a continuous exercise, which often becomes automatic.

First week: you need to talk with a medium-low volume, saying all you want. After a minute lower the tone, after another minute slow down the pace and then add breaks and smile.

Second week: the 5 minutes daily remain the same but you have to listen to a relaxing background music. In this phase the words must be chosen with care and the discussion must be built around 10 positive terms: pleasure, sweetness, well-being, beauty, trust and emotion.

Third week: repeat the exercises of the second week without preparing the speech, speaking freely. This time the words of well-being should be spontaneous.

THERE IS A TONE OF VOICE FOR EVERY SITUATION

Do you want to be nice?

Use the yellow voice, characterized by a big smile, constant and sincere. It is the voice of the radio speakers: friendly, smiling, friendly and always well-disposed towards everyone.

How can you create the yellow voice and in which situations can you use it?

We must use a medium-high volume, which must be associated with a smile that will be maintained for as long as we will continue to talk with that particular shade of color. For the tone of the voice, it will be alternately high and low depending on what will be exhibited (more acute in the excited phases and lower in the discursive phases). Speed will be sustained to generate in others that sense of energy and fun that is characteristic of nice people. Finally, breaks should be short.

Use it when the smiling approach will bring an advantage in communication (for example when you meet someone or when you start a public conversation).

Do you want to generate trust?

Use the green voice. After making yourself known through the yellow voice, you must create a relationship of trust with your partner. The green voice is the voice of that harmless person, of those who hold out the other cheek, of those who do not impose their personality but rather let the other choose them.

How can you create the green voice and in which situations can you use it?

The volume must be medium-low, an indication of your willingness to talk, rather than discuss. The tone must be low to give the impression of being calm and calm. Time will also have to be slow, because you are not in a hurry: you are relaxed and want to relax.

The pauses will be hesitant as proof that you are weighing the words. Use it in all those circumstances in which you intend to reach an agreement based on the sharing of values (it is the right item for teachers, ministers of religion, parents or politicians).

Do you want to be authoritative?

Use the blue voice, which will be effective if you have carried out the previous two steps accurately. The blue voice is very important to make people understand the elements of truth and reliability.

How can you create the blue voice and in which situations can you use it?

The volume will be medium-high and the tone will tend to be low and conclusive. Imparato writes: «The blue voice must lead the listener to think that the things we are saying are like carved in the rock: direct, safe, reliable and incontrovertible». The time must be medium, certainly not fast, sometimes slowed down in order to be able to scan more accurately the elements that you want to impress better in people's memory. As for the breaks, they must be clear, dry, suspensive.

The blue voice is especially useful when you need to communicate objective facts and data.

Do you want to get excited and involved?

Use the red voice, that of spontaneity, emotion and human warmth.

How can you create the red voice and in which situations can you use it?

First, the volume must be decidedly high, to make you feel, but above all, to convey your passion. The tone must be medium-high, because you are drawn by the topics you are facing. The time will be fast and the pace fast because you are conveying passion and enthusiasm.

Use the red voice whenever you want to involve those around you, to make it clear that it's time to start having fun. For this reason, it is not always usable but only in those cases in which the interlocutors are people with whom you have established a relationship of intimacy.

There are two colors that should never be used: gray and black.

The gray voice is that of boredom and apathy; the voice that is heard, unfortunately, in many public environments or among telephone operators; it is easily recognizable because it is dull, flat and expressionless.

The black voice, on the other hand, is the one of anger and hostility. It is the voice that is created when you discuss rather than talk. Its effects are really harmful for those who listen to it.

The paraverbal communication allows you to make yourself understood with your interlocutor. In fact, through paraverbale language, communicate your emotions, your moods and your intentions.

The mistake that is most frequently made when talking is to always use the same tone of voice to say everything. Especially in the professors we notice this error, which often talk about something exciting but they do it in the same way that they express something serious. There seems to be no difference, but if instead when they talk about something exciting they use the voice well with its characteristics, their message would surely come in a better way.

BODY LANGUAGE IS UNIVERSAL

Now I want to ask you something. So stop. Count to ten and try to clear your mind for a minute.

In what position were your hands the last time you talked to the grocery store? And what was the position of your feet when you accepted your current job? Do you remember facial gestures during your high school exam?

Not only words but also gestures, looks, postures act in communication. Knowing body language means knowing ourselves and others better, deciphering emotions and thoughts.

Communication is both verbal and non-verbal, it is made of what we say - so it is a conscious and wanted act - and of what we express with the body and face, often in an unconscious way.

What is the exact proportion between the verbal and non-verbal component within the discourse and how does one affect the other is still the subject of discussion.

Body language is a form of nonverbal communication. It is the part of communication that integrates, accompanies and sometimes contradicts verbal communication. We speak with words and gestures, with the tone of the voice and the expression of the face, with the movements and with the way in which we manage our personal space in relation to the objects that surround us.

However, the predominance of non-verbal communication seems to be undoubted. In short, expressions and gestures count more than words.

Understanding body language can help us better understand the mood and the real intentions of our interlocutor, helping us in everyday life: managing a job interview, a date or any other situation where you want make a good impression.

<u>Body language has always been considered as a channel through which to express oneself and one's identity.</u>

Non-verbal communication is the set of communicative elements that arise from the body and through which you can model communication and forward information to the listener. Everything happens through a personal style that is defined based on your most intimate emotions and essence.

THE POWER OF BODY LANGUAGE

Non-verbal communication is a very interesting area with different researches, more or less known, but unlike how it is presented by different authors, it is not an exact science. Just as words can have different meanings, even one's own gestures can be interpreted in different ways.

For example, crossing your arms can signal an attitude of closure, communicating anger but it can also simply indicate that the radiator is not working well.

Body language allows you to:

- Understand other people better
- Improve your relationship skills
- Understand the actual intentions of your interlocutor

What do you need to look to interpret non-verbal language?

Body language is extremely complex indeed it has been found that the human body is capable of producing over 700,000 different movements. Although almost all parts of the body can communicate, in this chapter we will focus on the 4 main areas:

1. Eyes
2. Face
3. Head
4. Posture

You probably noticed that when people think they tend to move their eyes. These shifts are not random but follow the particular type of internal cognitive process.

It may seem really strange but body language is an essential element in your journey to improve your social skills and overcome your social difficulties. Watch your hands, stamp your feet on the ground. Can you feel this great power you have inside you?

It is the fulcrum of an intense unconscious activity and if you learn to manage it you will have many more possibilities to look like anything you want.

The eye does not move randomly

You probably noticed that when people think they tend to move their eyes. These shifts are not random but follow the particular type of internal cognitive process. Now I want to give you a great gift. It's something I'm sure you'll find very useful. It is a special design that indicates the positions of the gaze and their hidden meanings. Read everything carefully and then I'll tell you two practical exercises to do to help you on your important path of growth and improvement.

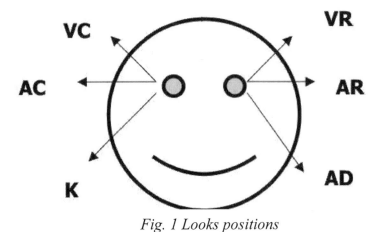

Fig. 1 Looks positions

VR- Visual Remembered (upper left eyes). Images previously seen are remembered.

What color are the sheets that are now in the bed?

How many balconies are there at your mother's house?

VC - Constructed Visual (upper right eyes). We build images never seen before.

Imagine a pink horse and a yellow mouse

Think of a city you've never been to

AR - Auditivo Remembered (eyes on the left side). We remember things heard earlier.

What's the last thing your neighbor told you?

What is the first verse of your favorite song?

AC - Building Audit (eyes on the right side). You create sounds never heard.

What would you answer if your cousin asked you if you want to adopt a Dalmatian dog?

How would a saxophone sound underwater?

AD - Digital Auditive (lower left eyes) This is the position of the internal dialogue.

How do you hear your voice when you speak internally?

K - Kinaesthetic (lower right eyes). In this position the eyes access emotions or bodily sensations.

Think of the feeling you get when you open the oven and the hot air comes out

How did you feel the last time you cried for a sad movie?

Attention: I want to reveal to you another element to learn about other people. Another parameter to consider when observing a person's eyes is pupil dilation. If your interlocutor's pupils are dilated there is a good chance that he is interested in you. In fact, dilated pupils can mean attraction, love, interest.

And now here are two practical exercises for you to learn to master your eyes and understand what the positions of the looks of the people you talk to mean.

Exercise n.1 - Go to the mirror and answer all the requests described above. Look closely at the look you have and the position of your eyes with each response. Then try to do it again by consciously managing the look, try to change the direction of the eyes and to invert the looks.

Exercise n.2 - Go out for three hours and talk to the people you meet: go to the supermarket, to work, get on the bus and ask for directions to strangers, go find a relative. Look closely at their looks and pay attention to yours.

Face is your emotions exhibit

Face is the most powerful tool with which we communicate non-verbally, it is a huge container of information and can tell us really a lot about who we face. We use the face to indicate when we are paying attention, to express emotions or even to try to hide them.

By carefully observing a face, you can also track down information about his personality, his attitude towards others and his state of health.

Facial expressions can be used to reinforce the message we are saying verbally or they can be in opposition to it and therefore communicate the complete opposite of what we are verbally saying (incongruity).

There are 7 basic emotions: sadness, surprise, anger, disgust, contempt, fear and happiness. They all have a corresponding facial expression that is transcultural and innate. Unlike gestures, which are rarely universal but vary depending on the culture and country of origin, the facial expressions that represent primary emotions are the same in all cultures and countries of the world. Not everyone knows that 43 facial muscles have been identified in the face that work at any given moment even when an emotion is temporary and we may not be aware of it.

Learn how to not lose your head!

Now let's talk about something really important: your head. In fact the head can send a wide variety of signals.

Head positions indicating listening

The most widely used head movement is "head nodtestading" (nod) which usually indicates interest in continuing the conversation and paying attention to listening. Many people actually nod their heads more frequently when they listen than when they talk.

But besides this there is another movement of the head that signals the listening this movement is called "head cock" and consists in tilting the head slightly on one side. This is a movement used very often by animals, especially by dogs, and also by children who use it when they try to attract attention to themselves. Tilting the head to one side can also signal sympathy and sweetness.

Touch the head

Touching the face can be a sign of anxiety or tension. People generally tend to have a favorite place to touch when they are worried. This is a behavior that poker players know well and they are very careful to observe in other players as they can signal if they have a good or a bad hand.

People can touch the side of the nose or caress the chin when they are thinking, making decisions or judging someone. Stroking oneself on the head can be a sign of self-punishment and therefore a sign of repentance, for example doing it on the forehead with the palm of the hand can mean "I'm stupid."

Head that does not move in any direction

The head often moves during conversation and this can signal submission or anxiety. When it does not move, it may indicate that the person is serious or is speaking from a position of superiority.

When the head is still and the eyes are not focused the person may not be attentive to the outside world, but rather be lost in their own thoughts and reflections.

The body speaks thanks to its posture

I invite you now to reflect on the posture you assume when you talk with other people. If you have any photos or videos on your mobile phone along with other people in convivial contexts, look at them carefully. Observe your posture. Are your shoulders curved? Is your abdomen in or out? How do you position your legs?

All the answers to these questions above are important. In fact, posture allows one to place oneself in a certain way with others and transmit sensations and nonverbal messages to people. Posture is linked to psychology in influencing emotional and cognitive processes. It allows us to recognize moods and influence our memory, decision making and metacognition abilities. In the embodied cognition approach the posture is very relevant for the close connection between mind and body. The term posture refers to the position of the human body in space and the relative relationship between its body segments. Posture can be: upright (monopodalic or bipodalic), sitting, decubitus (prone, supine, lateral).

The posture of an individual is the result of the person's own experience in the environment in which he lives, also determined by stress, physical and emotional traumas, incorrect postures repeated and maintained over time, incorrect breathing, biochemical imbalances derived from incorrect feeding, etc.

But how does posture bind to a good relationship with others?

Just as individuals are able to decode nonverbal communication signals of another kind, for example by interpreting the upward brow and the corners of the mouth downwards as a sign of sadness, in the same way they are able to associate certain postures with certain moods. For example: a person with very curved shoulders, almost closed in on himself, will transmit to the viewer a feeling of insecurity or fear; while those who assume an upright posture, with their back and shoulders straight and in line, will easily transmit the feeling of being a self-confident person.

To better understand yourself and others you must learn to recognize the universal types of postures.

Folded Posture

It is usually possible to observe this posture in very tall and thin-bodied people and who look like eternal adolescents, often with glasses because they are short-sighted. The body is folded, the shoulders curved, the chest hollowed and the head bowed forward. The feet seem to have little contact with the ground and the legs are so thin that they require the knees to stiffen to be able to support the body.

Characteristically they are people who have within them a great inner emptiness, probably due to a low maternal affection received during childhood and are people who tend to depend on others, even if this weakness is masked with extreme independence.

Posture divided into two parts

Characterized by a lean body and very tight muscles, feet turned outwards, the arms give way without giving signs of life and the face seems to have been cemented by its static nature.

He is a person with a very low self-esteem who has repressed his feelings since childhood, because he felt rejected as a human being. Even when engaged in romantic relationships, the individual who assumes this posture pretends to behave as if he were a very sentimental person, but in reality he is not.

Inflated posture

The upper body part is decidedly larger than the lower one, the chest is swollen, the neck is stretched, the rigid pelvis and the legs seem disproportionate to the body.

He is a person who denies his feelings a lot, in the sense that he really refuses their existence and prefers the idea of being able to control everything and everyone. Many times he arrives at important positions in the social sphere, but he needs to exercise his dominion over others, even if he eventually becomes dependent on the people he submits.

Submissive Posture

His body is crushed, so it is bigger, lower and stocky.

The neck is short and thick and the head seems to hide behind the shoulders, the pelvis is retracted and the buttocks are contracted.

He is a very childish character, because he thinks that only by behaving as others want he can be loved. He usually develops good muscles to keep his anger at bay and one of his greatest fears is that his anger comes out violently. Many times he feels hatred towards his boss or towards those who have a higher social position than his own.

Stiffness posture

The body is well proportioned, the head high, the neck stiff, the back straight and the chest swollen. It is the typical posture that soldiers take. He is an extremely rigid person and not very open to external stimuli, keeping his chest swollen indicates his rigidity. Probably during his childhood he was rejected by his parents and this caused him deep sadness.

Reading other people's body language is a complicated business. If someone crosses their arms, for example, you could assume that he is giving a signal to close, when he might just be cold. Having said that, when you try to understand what a person is really thinking, it helps to know which gestures and facial expressions you need to try to identify.

Because sometimes, the non-verbal manifestations of a person do not match perfectly with what he is saying in words.

Non-Verbal Communication is really very important, but we often do not consider how much we can use to reach our goals, in personal, emotional and professional fields.

70% of the impression others have of you comes from there. In fact, getting a good first impression on your interlocutor can help you look smarter or more likeable and ultimately have more friends and long-term social relationships.

Do you know that in the first minute of interaction with another person our body can emit up to 10,000 messages, almost completely unknowingly?

With the practice and self-observation of your gestures, you can use your gaze, posture, energy level and attitude to make a positive impression on others, especially in the first and crucial minute of conversation with them, but also in subsequent meetings.

Experts in this field even believe that the first 7-8 seconds are the most important in terms of impact. As you know, the first impression turns into a definitive judgment. Therefore, if in the first few seconds you have aroused a good impression on your interlocutor, there is a good chance that this will turn into a final judgment. Unfortunately, the opposite is also true. Body language communicates much more than the words we use. The slightest gesture, such as how we stand or enter a room, can reveal a great deal about our level of security, self-esteem and credibility. In practice, we can lie with words, but not with the body.

Here are some of the most effective body signals to gain attention, respect and confidence:

1. Adequate eye contact
2. Proper body position
3. Smile and nod
4. Proper posture

To improve the perception that people have of you, you can adopt the mirroring technique.

Mirroring is an indispensable technique that consists in imitating the movements of others, in order to tune into their own "wavelength", without people realizing it. Mirroring may seem an artificial thing, but in reality it is not, because we all, unconsciously, always use this technique when we interact with other people. Try to think about how we communicate when we need to interact with a child. We almost always lower ourselves and use a thin "voice" to talk to him. All this is the fruit of our unconscious that leads us to resemble the reference interlocutor, communicating in a similar way to his and helping us to get more in tune with the empathy.

If you have arrived here, you are halfway to your goal of improving your social skills. If you think that what you've read is something important to your life, something that really works, then I kindly ask you to leave a positive review on Amazon. This will allow me to continue writing interesting and useful books for all people.

LOVE AFFAIRS

Most timid individuals come to terms with making or receiving courtship with this character trait. This problem occurs both when the approach has the objective of presenting itself to determine the first moment of contact, and in the phases in which it is necessary to implement those behaviors aimed at being accepted as partners.

The basic problems suffered by shy people in such situations are mainly those of acceptance and competence.

The typology of negative automatic thoughts and behavioral behaviors vary according to the social role played in this particular type of two-way relationship, according to the beliefs that underlie these problems, and because of gender.

The basic beliefs that are generally activated in these cases are negative ones about oneself. These can be grouped into three categories:

1. Inadequacy ("I'm not up to par," "I'm a nerd," "I'm weak," "I'm a failure", "I'm a loser").
2. The unlovable ("I am boring /", "I have nothing to offer", "I am not a pleasant type", "I am defective").
3. Not being worthy of value ("I'm not able to love", "I'm useless", "I'm unacceptable", "I'm bad").

Also the type of expectations that the timid subject places towards the other vary according to the underlying beliefs.

For example, a woman who feels unlovable feels the need for repeated and continuous confirmations about the sincere feelings of the suitor, therefore she feels the need for a constant and long-term courtship. This is due to its great difficulty in confirming the belief that defines it as an unlovable person, in fact, it tends to consider the empathic behaviors of others, towards them, as if motivated by charitable or courtesy intentions.

If, on the other hand, we consider a male with the same type of belief, but who must act as a suitor, he feels the need for immediate acceptance, he lives the long time required and the feminine strategies based on the apparent lack of interest, as a demonstration of his not amiability and, therefore, his mind is pervaded by thoughts characterized by doubt, by the fear of not being appreciated.

A woman who has a basic problem of inadequacy, feels the courtship with the deep fear of not being able to know how to correspond or show, effectively, her own interest towards the other. This type of condition often leads to forward escaping behavior (facing the situation with high intensity of anxiety) followed then by blocking, embarrassing or even actual escapes.

A male who has the same type of problem, but has to act as a suitor, finds himself in great difficulty in reacting, promptly, to stimuli coming from the other. The state of anxiety of which he is pervaded drives him to focus his attention on himself or on the verification of any signs of rejection coming from the other. By continually posing the problem of "having to prove", and with the fear of not knowing how to do it, he often appears in obvious difficulty.

Hardly a social anxiety that has beliefs related to not feeling worthy of value, can interact with people of the other sex, when it does, risks being induced to detached or aggressive behavior. Considering it to be of little value, it considers the refusal on the part of others as a logical and inevitable consequence, therefore tends to anticipate what was expected, with its own refusal.

A common factor to all, regardless of the type of basic belief, remains the profound fear of the negative judgment of others.

Shy people or social anxieties in general, who have with anxiety and fear, the experience of an approach aimed at building a two-way relationship, live the post-situation with a great sense of dissatisfaction.

Their mind is devoured by brooding, often characterized by memories in the form of mental images. A very common judgment of oneself is the conviction of having given a bad impression.

People affected by shyness or other forms of social anxiety, in these contexts and in their inner dialogue a posteriori, do not take into consideration the positive elements, messages or appreciation signals that occur during the two-person interaction.

The attention of their brooding activity is inevitably oriented towards the confirmation of their negative beliefs.

FOR WOMEN WHO WANTS A MAN

Courting a man?

But isn't it a bad idea? Isn't it humiliating?

And then how is it done? Without appearing ridiculous, needy, desperate? Without sounding good?

Without devaluing yourself?

So let's take one step at a time.

Pursuing a man and losing the Trabzon every time you see him and behaving inconsistently and incoherently, search for him first, ask for his friendship on Facebook and then overwhelm him with "like" and chat, search for his phone number and contacting him, they are all attitudes that not only make you look like you were at the gas pipe, but they are in every way attitudes of who really is at the gas pipe.

Of those who do not value themselves, they do not know how to attract attention to themselves and do not want to seduce, but only fill gaps. In a clumsy and perhaps ridiculous way.

This way of doing things is counterproductive, because we convey the message that we are ready, very ready, extremely available to sell out. Many men of good will take into consideration the sale, the balance, the offer and in fact are looking forward to using women who behave in this way. Use and throw them.

This dynamic of cause and effect is also valid in other areas: if you do not value your work, you will be devalued by your colleagues as if you are your manager. And so it is also in friendships. Or in the family.

The devaluation of oneself in front of others entails another real risk, much more serious. That of devaluing even more in front of themselves, thus feeding a vicious circle. When I point out the importance of valuing oneself and not taking the first step or the first move, I am objected that we are no longer in the Middle Ages and that women are free to express their interest in the forms they prefer and otherwise give the idea of "feeling too cool" and then moving away from others rather than approaching them.

If you're wondering how to meet men in real life, there are five super simple tips that will help you meet someone you like and then conquer it.

Unlike films, most kids do not feel completely comfortable (or at least very good) in meeting women in real life. When they see you they feel embarrassed, uncertain what to say, they are ashamed.

The five suggestions I will give you are based on the simple idea that men want to meet you: you just have to give them clearer signals and better opportunities.

1. Create free time.

I know this may seem obvious, but if you're guilty of being constantly late and super busy, don't be surprised if you don't meet anyone. Regardless of the fact that you are too busy looking at your phone, to see if there is someone nice around you, men interpret your frenzy as if you were unapproachable. Being super busy means not seeing opportunities and men will avoid interrupting you. Try to change this, and note the difference that this entails.

2. To make this more effective, you need to keep the phone in your purse.

Even if you are simply scrolling through Instagram, a man will interpret this again as a "she is busy" signal and will not commit to approaching you. The same applies if you wear headphones. So it's time to change and have a little awareness. Phone down. Earphones away.

3. The other piece of the puzzle is to make sure you get its attention.

This does not mean that you have to drastically change your personal style, but it does mean that when you enter a place, you do not just hide in the corner of the room immediately until someone arrives. Instead, I'd like you to walk around the room. When you go out, choose a place like a bar, a club, a pub etc ... a place where there are lots of opportunities to meet new people. You can also give men a way to start a conversation using something that is easy to comment on. It is often much easier for him to say that he likes your hat, necklace, sweater rather than saying that he finds you attractive. So it might be time to find that boldest accessory or red cap that will make you the bait to look good and try.

4. Approach him.

Let's be honest, even if you wear a shirt that says 'approached', some men might still not understand. I know you could say, I want to go out only with a man who has the courage to approach me. But just because a man isn't approaching you at that moment doesn't mean he's not a good man.

He could indeed be such a caring man that he didn't find the right time to get close to you. To help him, approach him. You can reduce your fear by approaching them if you are interested. This could be anywhere, in the supermarket queue, in a bar or next to them, in a yoga class, etc.

5. Now imagine that you are within walking distance of a cute man.

To complete your clear signal checklist to encourage him to come closer, I want you to focus on eye contact with him and the smile. I know it sounds easy, but I also noticed that in many women, the first reaction when they see a man they like is to look at him steadily. Only some eye contact (look at it, look elsewhere, look back) and smiling shows that you are open to talk to him and make him understand your availability.

Sometimes seducing an exceptional man may seem like a marathon, but if you can stay positive, active and open to all the different ways of meeting men in real life, the journey becomes much more fun.

Do you like a boy but he is shy and you can't break down his barriers? Try following these suggestions.

Shyness is only the side effect of a precious gift that must be appreciated and protected: sensitivity.

You found the perfect boy, the one that makes your heart beat and that makes you melt with every smile. Everything seems perfect, apart from a small problem: he is shy and he can't come forward!

1. Spend time with him "as a friend"

Shy boys are often stronger and more confident with their friends, while with a girl who could become their girlfriend they tend to shut themselves up and try to avoid it.

By offering yourself to him as a friend, not only will you have the opportunity to get to know him more easily, but he will feel that he can lower his guard with you gradually and, slowly, you will be able to pass from friend, to best friend, to girlfriend.

2. Manage conversations with him

With a shy boy the conversation plays a much more important role than what happens with a more open and confident person.

Be proactive and push him to open up by asking questions about topics that might interest him.

In this way you will take away from him the weight of having an interesting conversation with you and make him feel at ease. To do this, however, remember that even if you manage the topics, you will have to start a conversation that really interests you and where you can participate as soon as you feel like it.

You can for example start by talking briefly about your hobbies and then ask them which ones are yours. Find what he cares about most and encourage him to always talk about it through questions. A pleasant and stress-free conversation is a great way to get to the heart of a shy person.

3. Read his body language

If he hides how he feels and what he feels, you will have to find out. If he doesn't offer you topics to talk about, try to wander through various topics that may interest a man and, through his look, find out when you hit the mark on his.

For a shy person, in fact, it is very important that within the relationship his girlfriend manages to understand him without having to face an argument. The more we understand it, the more he will be able to open up and overcome his shyness.

4. Train your memory

If you want to conquer a shy boy, you will need to have an exceptional memory. Every detail will be important: the name of his parents, the name of his dog, how much sugar he takes in coffee. The more you know him, the less he will have to repeat the details of his life, the more he will feel involved and tied to you. As if I've known him forever. A shy boy needs to feel secure.

5. Talk to him about yourself

Talk to him about you. Tell them about your little details (a mole, a small scar you made as a child, etc.) and some of your secrets. He will feel much more at ease when he knows you so "intimate" and will be free to let go without fear.

6. Keep secret what it tells you

If you trust yourself, no matter how small things may be and you may seem "to be told", don't talk about it with anyone.

If, for example, he tells you that he went to run on Saturday morning, it may not seem like a secret to keep, but it is not said that he also talked about it with his friends. If, for example, they were to ask him where he is going to run because you let slip this detail of his life, he could feel "betrayed" by the trust he gave you.

Once betrayed the trust of a shy person, the situation could hardly be recovered.

7. Organize the outputs

Never leave a shy person in charge of organizing an exit together (unless he proposes himself). He could panic and delay organizing and leaving, or he could choose more suitable outlets for you than him to please you.

Be the one to go to meet him. It organizes outings in contexts that can suggest topics for conversation (for example cinema, theater, an exhibition, etc.) and avoids those in which breaks and silences can be "embarrassing" (for example in a pub or at a restaurant for dinner, in ice cream shop, etc.)

He will not have the "anxiety" of organizing an exit and, above all, he will feel very comfortable with you because you will have chosen places where he can relax and where he cannot feel uncomfortable.

Sooner or later even the most "interesting" releases will arrive, you just need to respect his times.

8. Introduce him to friends and relatives with caution

It is not necessary for him to know all your friends and your whole family immediately.

For example, if you have friends who are too "impetuous" or relatives with too much character, wait before you become great friends and a close-knit couple.

If you really can't wait, before taking it with you to them, you will all be aware of the fact that he is shy and observes their reactions. There are those who understand the situation and will help them get comfortable and there are those who will laugh. Make it known only to those who are sensitive enough to let them have a good time.

HOW TO DATE A MAN

In a world like today, where perhaps the essence of the purest love has been lost, it is important to at least give the right importance to the phase of courtship, the most beautiful and purest phase of a story.

However, it is not always easy for a woman to understand the rules and allow herself to be courted: in a society that invites the fairer sex to be always strong, detached and "masculine", the confusion can be so much about what it can mean to be courted.

The first phase of courtship is that of seduction.

Most women expect men to take the first step and rightly so it is right. However too many women have a wrong perception of men and consequently too high expectations: men are not all bold, and for the more timid it can be really difficult to come forward.

There are men, even very attractive, extremely insecure that maybe because of this they develop a kind of block and have not had a woman in years. Hence, if a mutual interest is perceived, sometimes it may be necessary to encourage a deepening of knowledge.

"Incentive" does not mean to be available immediately in sexual terms or to put oneself wrong but simply to make the other person understand that you are also interested.

The key is to show off discreetly, always with a lot of class. It will be enough to wander around him and maybe, why not, even exchange a few words.

In this way you will help him break the ice, melt a little and take courage. Keep in mind that the fear of rejection in humans is very strong, a rejection affects pride, virility.

If the man is shy then, this fear is multiplied by at least five.

The advice is, be reassuring, let him understand that with you that risk does not exist and that the desire to know each other is mutual. If he is really interested, success is assured, in this way you will help him bring down his insecurities and fill him with courage to take the next step. If, on the other hand, the other party reacts presumptuously, simply move away, or you will most likely regret it soon.

If the first glances, movements and words have been successful, then we move on to the real dialogue phase. In this case, the subject is not as important as the tone, the way in which we start talking, the gestures. Don't misunderstand, content is extremely important and finding a person who is challenging and intriguing especially on a mental level is one of the basic requirements once the relationship is more "initiated".

flirt However, the very first dialogue can and must almost keep on trivial and superficial issues, so as to keep one's private sphere protected: you still have no idea who you are facing, better to play safely.

Rather, at this stage, pay attention to how it moves, the body has its own language and the movements reveal much of a person's thoughts.

Another key point, smile. The smile will be the most important element of all in the first approach. Laughing together will help ease the tension and break the ice, causing both to feel less embarrassed.

If you feel safe and have good feelings, you can decide later, to introduce more personal themes, perhaps sharing more private anecdotes or expressing a more precise opinion about a more important topic than the gin and tonic you are sipping or fact that "there are no more mid-seasons". This will ensure that the couple reaches greater intimacy and that the ice melts almost permanently. Do not expect to feel immediately at ease: for a woman it takes some time and many encounters before being able to genuinely trust the man she has in front, even when it comes to the perfect man.

At this point, however, you can trigger the last stage of courtship, or that of physical contact, but it will have to happen randomly, an arm touched by chance, a hand on the shoulder. From the other person's reaction to these small gestures you will understand if the interest is real. At this point you have done your part, let man bring everything to the next level.

FOR MEN WHO WANT TO DATE A WOMAN

"I'm a disaster, I can't have dates with girls."

How many times have you repeated these phrases to yourself? You did it so much that you convinced yourself to suffer from shyness. It could also be true, but you can stop doing it, you can literally break down shyness with women and the good news is that you can start right away!

If you want to stop being shy towards girls, in this book you can find three simple strategies that you can start using today.

First, avoid these wrong strategies.

On the internet you will find a lot of information on shyness towards girls and how to overcome it, but they are totally wrong.

When I was shy with girls, I remember reading things like "Don't talk too much. Listen and let me talk" or "What's the worst thing that can happen?"

<u>These are all absolutely wrong tips if you want to overcome shyness.</u>

That kind of advice would be nice for someone who has a tendency to talk so much, but they are dramatically wrong with a shy person who already speaks little of his.

What about the guy who can't get close to a girl and talk to her because she feels too nervous? What about the guy who is smart enough to know that nothing really bad can happen, but he still feels that overwhelming anxiety that stops him every time?

Finally I realized that most of the people who wrote this stuff had never been shy about the girls themselves, they had just pulled out a web page to earn some money.

The boys, or at least most of them, feel a little nervous near the girls they are attracted to, they are able to breathe deeply, to talk and to feel at ease over time. All pretty normal stuff.

This unfortunately does not happen to those who suffer from shyness with girls.

And it is to you that I want to address today, to those boys who feel really anxious and scared, inhibited by girls.

I will teach you to overcome shyness through three basic steps:

1. overcome inferiority
2. don't be obsessed with just one girl
3. become assertive.

Negative thoughts like "I'm too shy with girls" will only be a distant memory and you can begin to concretely solve your shyness problem with girls.

A primary cause of shyness with girls is a feeling of inferiority. If you feel somehow "less precious" than the girl, then you will feel shy and nervous around her.

Here is a simple example that will help you understand better.

Imagine an overweight or unattractive girl you know. Do you feel any anxiety or nervousness when you are near her? No, probably not. And if you do, it will certainly be much less than close to the girl you are attracted to.

Now think about the way you talk to girls you are not particularly attracted to. Aren't you more relaxed and relaxed with them? Don't you talk to them the same way you would talk to a friend?

Instead, in front of a girl that you find attractive, your mind suddenly becomes empty and you can't think of anything anymore, you don't know what to say.

Why does it happen? Why are you shy only for certain girls? This happens when so much importance is attributed to the appearance of a beautiful girl to the point of intimidating you.

Your excessive shyness with women therefore does not concern all women, but only some, precisely the girls you are attracted to and who consider them to have greater aesthetic value.

So if you think you suffer from shyness with women and you're wondering how to get out of it, start with this starting point: the solution is, of course, to stop attributing so much value to appearance.

Treat an attractive girl in the same casual and natural way that you would treat an unattractive friend or girl. Sure, you might be more attracted to a good looking girl, but the physical appearance alone shouldn't be enough to make you intimidated and conquered immediately.

I remember when I was very shy with girls when I fell in love with a woman I began to fantasize about our future together without ever really talking to her!

In hindsight, it seems so silly, yet so many shy kids do it. They become infatuated with a girl based on how she looks from a distance, based on her appearance.

They haven't talked to her yet, yet they begin to imagine a future with her.

<u>There are lots of pretty girls in the world, but it's rare to find a girl you can have fun with and have a personality that is compatible with yours.</u>

Don't put the girl on a pedestal before you even know her, treat her like a human being like you, not like a goddess.

That's why so many women give kids the advice to "be themselves". They don't like it when a guy tries to impress and convince them to like it, especially when they don't know each other and they haven't done anything to deserve attention, apart from looking nice

Realize that a person's appearance does not determine how valuable it is or how much it is worth. Being good-looking is more fortunate in having the right genes. Would you think for example that a lottery winner is superior to you? It's about luck.

Another way to feel inferior is to think that being less experienced than a girl in relationships makes you immediately repulsive.

When I was shy, I remember thinking that I had to "hide" the fact that I never had a girlfriend. I thought that if the girl realized by the way I acted that I was inexperienced or that I was sexually so, then she would get up and leave automatically.

The truth is, if you take this kind of attitude, if you feel undeserving towards the more experienced girls, then you're just sabotaging yourself. At the risk of wearing a shy and reserved mask that is unlikely to be appreciated

If you grew up in shyness and have always been shy with girls, then it will be almost inevitable that most girls will have more experience than you.

To "recover", to start being less shy with girls you need to start talking more and try to get involved.

This is really a great prospect to have: the fact that you have less experience than the average does not mean that girls don't like you. It just means that you have to make up for some lost time due to your shyness or social anxiety. You started later than anyone else. And this brings me to the last point, the third mistake you make is the basis of your shyness problem with girls.

Inferiority makes you feel that you don't have the right to trust yourself, you feel like you can't express your personality.

A big problem that you should overcome is your thoughts. Many shy people have a constant stream of negative thoughts, they constantly repeat themselves as losers and constantly mull over the past.

If you constantly think about why you are a loser, like the fact that you are not handsome, that you have some physical defect to be solved, that you are a loner with few or no friends, or if you think you never even kissed a girl, then you're just sabotaging yourself, once again!

By being too hard on yourself and being unsure about your appearance, you are constantly reinforcing the idea in your mind that you are inferior to the girl you like best.

This makes it IMPOSSIBLE for you to be confident next to you, because you think it is more valuable. And if you lack confidence and can't even talk to her normally, then you have no chance of attracting her and forming a relationship.

Then you must be wondering, "how to succeed with girls?"

I answer you with a very simple sentence: trust and personality are more attractive than the physical appearance for most girls, your looks don't count as much as you think they do. If you don't believe me, then look around: all good-looking girls are around confident, popular and charismatic kids.

On the other hand, many of the good guys who are shy are "stuck" in a relationship with a girl they are not particularly attracted to. Being good-looking is much more important for girls than boys.

So the most important thing to overcome shyness with women is to eliminate any thoughts that can sabotage your self-confidence to the point of inhibiting yourself. This means noticing when you're having this kind of self-destructing thoughts, you have to stop them in the bud.

Any thoughts that make you feel less precious will only sabotage your progress in becoming less shy with girls.

Observe when they occur, challenge them with the ideas you have learned so far and instead try to focus on your good qualities of which you are proud. Remind yourself that girls are not really looking for the most beautiful boy, but for those who can be self-confident and strive to talk to girls without being intimidated by their superficial qualities.

Do you find yourself choosing a girl you like and then thinking for hours about how it would be to go out with her and have a relationship with her?

Maybe the girl showed you some interest ... Maybe you just talked to her once for a couple of minutes ... Or maybe she's in your class and you never said a word to her before.

If you constantly stare at one girl at a time and play with the fantasies in your head, what it would be like to go out with her, then you're sabotaging yourself again.

What do you think happens when you decide to finally want to talk to the girl in real life? You're too nervous to move. You've been thinking about it for so long and you've built it in your mind like a creature so perfect that it literally becomes paralyzed with fear.

Now do you understand why you feel too shy with girls?

Meanwhile, the girl may not even be aware that you exist.

All the thoughts you have built make you unable to get close to her and speak to her in a natural way. And even if you do, the way you behave next to her tells her again that you would be totally crushed if she disapproved of you in some way or rejected you.

The problem is that you let yourself be too emotionally involved with the girl before she did something to get your attention. You spent so much time thinking about her that her refusal would ruin your imaginative image of you two together.

But this relationship does not really exist except in your head. The sooner you understand it the better.

So what do you do to be less shy with girls?

Don't have too many expectations.

One thing especially of shy kids is that they can talk to an attractive girl for a few seconds and then give too much importance to interaction. They could start fantasizing about the girl, do everything to meet her.

The key to avoiding this problem and succeeding with girls is to establish relationships with them without a secret agenda in which they are consecrated as the only love of life!

<u>Don't have too many expectations about a future relationship with a particular girl until you spend a fair amount of time getting to know her.</u>

Until you have known someone for a period of time, you have no idea what it really is. That girl you think is perfect could be boring, she could be insecure despite being beautiful, she could be completely lacking in intelligence, disappointing in short.

And if you don't know it, then you will never notice that you were only seeing it with different eyes

Boys who have little experience in the relationship tend to be naive and think that most relationships develop as a romantic Hollywood movie: two people fall in love with each other when they see each other for the first time.

It is a situation that often happens in introverted people

The reality is very different. Long-term relationships develop over time and are always evolving, learning to know how to wait.

One way to stop being so obsessed with a particular girl is to have many options instead of just one choice. The best way to do this is to talk to many women a week or even every day. If you only talk to a new girl a month, it will be hard not to think about her.

But if you constantly meet new girls, it becomes much easier to see her as a girl you talked to once and that's it.

Now I want to tell you something very important that you will never forget:

DESTINY DOES NOT EXIST

Many inexperienced kids with women have misconceptions about how relationships work. Perhaps you also think that the best strategy to succeed with women is to wait for the right circumstances.

Are you waiting for a situation where you happen to meet a girl, magically you're not nervous talking to her, don't you have to ask her out and do all the moves? It's like waiting for the stars to line up forming a heart pierced by an arrow.

The hard reality is that you will have to work and learn to deal with your nervousness if you want to have a girlfriend. The universe will not deliver you one.

Of course, you might be lucky a couple of times when a girl commits to meet you, talks to you and takes the initiative. But it probably won't be the girl you want. If you want something, you have to chase it, the boys are the ones who make the moves!

In our society, or perhaps because of our biological programming, it is the children who need to be isolated about meeting new girls and establishing relationships with them.

And let me say that this is right.

Do not hesitate!

Being assertive is like a muscle. The more you do it, the less effort it takes.

When you try to kiss a girl for the first time, or walk and talk to a girl, you'll probably hesitate a little, you'll stop. Then when you try to do it again, after a couple of minutes, your "mental barrier" to act becomes higher.

It becomes even more difficult to "just do it".

And the longer you think about whether you should make your move or not, the more anxious you feel. It's like when you think of a girl for months and it becomes impossible to talk to her, you built it in your mind so much that you became a victim of paralysis through analysis.

Instead, more action is needed on that first impulse. That first impulse is your best shot to actually do it. Everything you think about later is used to stop it.

If a girl refuses your kissing attempt, all you have to do is smile and keep talking to her normally. Then try again after ten minutes: many times the girl does not refuse you, she simply does not feel at ease at that moment.

If you talk to a girl and she doesn't like you, then don't start thinking about how to conquer her. There are literally billions of

girls out there, just find another one, just so you can overcome shyness with girls.

Be resolute, act and stop self-sabotaging yourself, not only will you win shyness with girls but you'll love yourself more.

FRIENDS AND COLLEAGUES

We spend most of our time at work, more than we spend with our family or loved ones, we work side by side with other people for 8 hours, we share good days and bad days, successes and disappointments, we collaborate to a common purpose. In this situation, it is desirable to establish peaceful relations with our colleagues and in some cases it is normal to see friendships that go beyond the walls of the office arise. A joke in front of the coffee machine, a lunch break together, a business meeting are all occasions that let us get to know our colleagues better until we consider them friends.

Certainly, having friends at work has advantages in terms of psychological well-being and professional development. The workplace is not only an environment where we share spaces, but also a place full of negative and positive emotions. Having friendly presences gives us more energy and motivation to face our days and a shoulder to lean on in the darkest days. Even sharing the extra work problems (eg small children, etc.) one feels understood without needing so many explanations. But they are not all roses.

Sometimes, in fact, what appears to be a friendship, turns out to be a relationship based on interest. You can show solidarity and collaboration but it can happen to find yourself in situations that are not pleasant enough to turn your face to your friend / colleague. That's why workplace friendship is one of the most delicate issues to deal with.

Here are 6 tips to manage friendships at work.

1. Don't isolate yourself from others

Having a relationship of complicity with a colleague can lead you to not consider and exclude other colleagues - seen almost as a threat to this special relationship. The risk is to isolate yourself from others and create tension. Some colleagues may be jealous of this complicity and try to sabotage it. Be aware of this and try to have a peaceful and friendly relationship with all your colleagues. Attention also to the language: express yourself to the positive - avoiding to speak ill of others - and contribute to maintaining a pleasant atmosphere.

2. Keep the focus

Having friends at work can increase motivation and also our productivity if we are able to keep the focus on work. The risk is in fact being easily distracted by the chatter and forgetting the projects we are following to then find ourselves having to run to recover. Be professional and meet deadlines, don't let yourself be distracted by too many coffee breaks. A lunch or an aperitif after work is a way to spend time with your friend / colleague without compromising productivity.

3. Communicate directly and clearly

When a problem arises at work, don't be afraid to say things exactly as they are. This will avoid quarrels that could damage your professional and personal life. As I write in Free Your Life about the commissioner's trap that always looks for the culprit, telling the truth is one thing; the way it is said is another. The idea is not to keep quiet and to let the error go. Consider how to formulate communication so that the other person feels appreciated and not blamed. You can start by explaining your reasons. For example, to say: "I appreciate our professional (and personal) relationship and I would like to see it grow and, for that to happen, I need to talk to you about a difficult issue for me". We can point out errors without falling into arrogance, criticism or blame. We can be hard on the problem by staying soft with the person.

4. Don't take it personally

Similarly, when we receive a critique, the best attitude is to remind ourselves that it is our way of thinking, our phrase, our action, our project to be judged, criticized or attacked. Not necessarily us. The criticism is towards the idea that the person has of us. So it has little to do with us and a lot to do with the person who is refusing / attacking / criticizing us at that time. There is a big difference between the thought they have of us and who we really are!

A clear distinction must be made between person and behavior. We as persons are more than our projects, our actions and even our thoughts. To avoid personalizing when we are under attack, we need to train the detachment: detachment helps us to stop dramatizing and take things more lightly.

5. Attention to ambition

How to do it when one of the two receives a promotion and goes up a level? If our friend becomes our superior, the risk of falling into the trap of the judge who makes constant comparisons is high. As I write in Free Your Life, we try to consider our friend / colleague an incentive to inspire us to improve ourselves. Ask yourself: what are the qualities present in this person that I want to increase in me? What can I do to achieve that result? How can I do it respecting myself?

6. Set some limits

Do you work better in an orderly space? Do you need to focus in silence before an important appointment? Does it bother you to be continually interrupted by your colleague's questions? Or vice versa, do you often need to brainstorm with someone about the projects you are following at work? It is important to learn to communicate your needs. In fact, to work at its best, everyone needs to enforce their personal space. And to do so, the first step is to know ourselves well (which is not so obvious) and our reactions.

Life is too short to be unhappy, even in the workplace. How many of us can claim to feel happiness at work? Aren't we always stressed, distressed, angry, scared or bored? The leaders who do not respect us, the colleagues who do not seem to share your own emotions, an office that is too chaotic, the injustice of some hierarchical dynamics. But then we tell ourselves what does it matter? You don't have to be happy at work, after all it's just work.

But the truth is that nobody wants to live like this: being happy in the office, or any workplace where we spend about 8 hours a day, is as important as being happy in our free time. Work and personal life are not so far apart.

We are always there, valid for everyone: relationships are difficult. And not only the intimate ones with the partner, even the professional relationships, with superiors and colleagues, or even with friends. "Man is not an island", it is his nature to seek relationships with others, but it is often very complicated to deal with people other than themselves. We can often clash due to differences of opinion or interest, and sometimes we risk to send a friendship, a love, a good working relationship, due to unresolved misunderstandings.

Also there is another thing you need to think about. Work is an important component of your life and having solid relationships in a professional context allows you to feel greater confidence in yourself in all the other contexts of your life.

Being ambitious is not a defect. On the contrary: at some point in our career - after having invested talent, time and energy in carrying out projects that have contributed to the growth of the company we work for - it is legitimate that we aspire to achieve something more. And not only because a more rounded salary would make us face life with more serenity, but also because it would give us the charge to continue doing well. And to believe that those who commit themselves the most are meritoriously valued. Of course, this is the ideal situation: one that does not take into account the incorrectness and favoritism that characterize certain work environments, but let us strive to be positive. And to think that, to get a career advancement, it is enough to get busy and demonstrate how much we are worth. In short, it needs to be appreciated more every day. Yeah, but how do you do it?

Let us remember that, even (and above all) at work, the exams never end. What does it mean? That even if we have set foot in the company for a long time and we have earned the respect and esteem of everyone (or almost), we cannot lower our guard. Because the eyes of those who are paid to judge our work and entrust us with any growing responsibilities continue to observe us very carefully. Whoever aspires to obtain a career advancement cannot disregard it or underestimate the fact that other colleagues also aim to be noticed by the boss. We must not frame the issue as a struggle without exclusion of blows, but as a healthy competition on equal terms. Which - in the usual ideal situation that we are hypothesizing - will end up rewarding the most deserving. That is the one (or the one) who will succeed in being appreciated more. Working hard is only the beginning: if we want to strengthen our chances of making a career, we must do our best and concentrate on these things:

1. Show reliability

No boss will ever consider promoting an employee he does not trust. Even if it was the most capable and brilliant that ever happened to him. Leaders are often forced to delegate and cannot think of leaving the company helm (even for short periods) to unreliable people, who do not show sufficient dedication and involvement. It works exactly as in private life: none of us would ever dream of entrusting our most precious asset to a forgetful and distracted person. As charismatic or friendly as it may be. Why should our superior do so, that by choosing to entrust us with responsibilities, he risks losing a lot? Gaining the trust of the boss does not mean always giving him reason, but showing him that we work for the good of his company, devoting the right attention and due consideration to everything we do.

2. Let us be determined and responsible

The longer you go on in your career, the more you have to make delicate decisions. Are we ready to do this? If we want to play a greater role in the company, we have to deal with our ability to manage situations and people, which can create many problems. To be appreciated more and more, we must show ourselves to be determined and enterprising. Because there are leaders (and perhaps ours is one of these) who prefer to passive and compliant employees those who propose plans and suggest solutions. If we have ideas and enthusiasm to support them, we start off on the right foot. But what makes the difference could be our willingness to take responsibility, even when things are not going well. Everyone knows how to stay on board, when the sea is calm and navigation proceeds peacefully; but whoever does not abandon the ship, when the waves are high, deserves another consideration.

3. We share successes with others

Needless to turn around: if the management is thinking of promoting someone, we will be taken into consideration, only if we have brought home the results. Because, in the usual ideal situation that we are outlining, only the employees who deserve it can aspire to obtain a career advancement. We can prove our validity also in this case and make ourselves appreciated for the way in which we choose to celebrate the successes, which should certainly not be underestimated or diminished. Those who flaunt themselves, flaunting their merits at every turn, demonstrate that they have not reached an appreciable level of professional maturity. While those who have learned to share successes with others and know how to recognize the merits of the people who helped them make goals, show that they are ready to move forward. Let us commit ourselves not to be self-centered and to reason in a perspective of constant and fruitful collaboration.

If we have been dreaming of occupying an important role in the company for a long time, we must do our utmost. Betting on our skills, our fairness and complete dedication to work. Let us show that we are ready to take on our responsibilities, let us look around and surround ourselves with the right people (avoiding stepping on those who don't like us or those who aspire to make a career like us). With these references, the possibility of toasting our promotion soon will no longer seem so remote.

HOW TO LOOK NICE

Now let's talk about something you don't like at all. You think you are a brilliant person, nice with so many smart things to say but when the time comes you never have the right words and think you are an idiot.

Tell the truth: you are an intelligent person who does well in life, but when it comes to breaking the ice with a person or starting a conversation or when you come face to face with a man you like, your self-esteem plummets at abysmal levels and do you find it very difficult to be nice?

Quiet: it is a problem common to many, both men and women. It is not easy to be nice: you know that it is easier to be casual during a university exam for which you have prepared yourself or for a question at school (do you know?) Rather than in a short, one-on-one conversation with a person who did you just meet? Especially if you find it interesting and want to impress.

There is good news: you can learn to be nice and you can do it in a simple and fun way for you, discovering many things about your true personality and the behavior of others. This is very useful when it comes to winning over a man and creating a strong and lasting relationship.

What makes you nice?

Meanwhile, a bit of ready-to-use culture: sympathy comes from the Greek sim-patheia, which is a compound word that means "feeling emotions with the other person". Being "nice" means being able to tune into each other for what concerns joy, but also the pain, fun, joy, concentration and all the infinite range of emotions that a person feels.

Even - you feel a little - the excitement and sexual tension. Not as bad as what: sympathy is the basic ingredient of sexual attraction, it is a fundamental component for triggering the spark between two people...

Not only: sympathy is a relational skill whose seed that can be "planted" within itself, cultivated and made to grow. Just want it and you just need to follow some small rules, to receive immense rewards from your life with others. What do you say, have you decided to find out how to be nice? It could be one of the most "transformative" experiences of your existence.

3. Encourage the other to speak. How? Asking him questions about him. Think about it: is there a more interesting topic of conversation than talking about yourself? Certainly not, especially for the male human being.
4. Ask questions: for example, if he talks about his last holidays in the Canary Islands, ask him: "How are the Canaries? What did you eat?". Asking "interesting" (non-intrusive) questions makes you be nice and makes you remember.
5. Use body language to show that you are focused on the man you are talking to - not because he is handsome or rich or because you are desperate for a man, but because you are interested in him as a person, because you really want to enter

in "connection" with him -. Show them with your eyes and eye contact (look into his eyes with interest and sweetness) that you are really listening to him and that you are talking to him and not to the wind or to an imaginary interlocutor or - worse than worse - to yourself. Keep your arms extended and your body in an "open" posture, always facing you. Being nice with your whole body makes you extremely attractive, without forcing you to act or sell yourself out.

6. Learn to speak and learn to keep quiet. Again: pay close attention to the people in front of you. To all people, not just to the man you want to conquer. Being nice doesn't mean giving yourself to do to please only those who attract you, but to be attentive to the needs and sensitivities of everyone you deal with. Do you believe that an intelligent and interesting man does not notice the fact that you are unpleasant with everyone and then with him you become a lamb of availability and sweetness? Do you believe that a man who knows his stuff does not weigh the falsity of such behavior? You're wrong. Being nice is an inner attitude of love and true collaboration towards others.

Speak clearly and uniformly. Start by trying to keep the tone and volume as constant as possible. If you often scream or whisper you may seem less intelligent. Also, to make what you say clearer, you'll need to make sure you don't talk too fast. You will also have to be careful not to mumble. Speaking the words well will make you look a lot smarter. Few things make a silly person look more like using words incorrectly or uttering bad words. This often happens with the most complex words, in particular if you are trying to look smarter using refined terms that you still don't understand well. Just use the words you really know.

Avoid interlayers. These are the words you say when you are trying to think of what to say next. We all use interlayers, even if we don't notice them. These are words like "umm," "ahh," "eeh," "ie," "I mean," and others like it. The interlayers are often different for each region and language, but their effect is always the same: you give the impression of thinking slowly and it is difficult to understand what you have just told.

If you are having a conversation or attending a meeting and want to look smarter, ask questions. Sounds strange to you, right? But if you ask the right questions in the right way, you will make it clear that you are thinking intelligently about what has been said. Think about the questions that show you are looking at long-term goals or the reasoning behind actions. Think about the questions that show you are trying to understand a complex system more thoroughly. These are the questions that make you look smart.

SIX PRACTICAL EXERCISES TO IMPROVE SELF-CONFIDENCE

Interpersonal relationships are not easy, but sometimes they are easier than you think. Some people are unable to interact with others adequately because of shyness, while others are brought into conflict, perhaps for a family environment where there have never been good relationships. This gives rise to and continue over time controversies that do not lead to anything good or distrust and concern for others.

The ability or inability to establish good personal relationships is not innate: it is true that there are some genetic predispositions that make us more or less extroverted, more or less sociable, but this is not decisive. In reality, we learn to interact adequately with others. To do this, it is necessary to develop some skills that are available to everyone.

We can also use some tricks to simplify this learning. These are small steps that are very easy to implement and effective in our purpose of improving interpersonal relationships.

TRY TO TRAIN LISTENING SKILLS

The listening activity is not limited - it should not - to shut up while the other spells out. It goes much further: it means turning our attention to the content and form of the message that the other tries to get us. It is not a question of remaining silent, but of following part of a journey that leads us to connect to what the other person says, suggests or insinuates. It is not even a question of silencing our inner dialogue, but of directing it towards what they are telling us.

To develop the ability of listening, there is nothing better than listening. But then, how? Let's try to remain silent, simply trying to capture what they tell us. Initially it will be necessary to make a conscious effort so that our attention does not diminish, after having taken our hand, however, the temptation to ramble will not be so strong.

Practical Exercise: your annotation notebook.

Go to the stationery shop and buy a notebook, a nice notebook that you really like. I recommend you choose one you really like because this notebook will be essential. In fact you will have to use it twice a day (at noon and in the evening before going to bed) to write down the important things that people have told you during the day. Then put a red ball next to the things you answered with real interest, a blue ball to the things you listened to without being involved, a green ball to the things you didn't hear well. Think carefully about everything you write and find a way to be more involved.

IMPLEMENT EMPATHY

Active listening and empathy go hand in hand. Turning all our attention to the message they are trying to convey allows us to understand it according to the context of the other person and not according to ours. Empathy is precisely this: being able to put yourself in others' shoes understanding the process that causes them to think and act according to their own criteria.

Empathy therefore requires an open rather than critical attitude. We are all unique and do what we do for reasons that often escape us. With what right can we put ourselves to review? In this sense, you lose a lot when you don't get to establish empathy. Learning, growth and the opportunity to improve interpersonal relationships are lost.

Empathy is the ability to understand and share the feelings and emotions of another person. It is an essential ability to build good relationships, both at work and in personal life. People who do not show empathy are considered cold and self-absorbed and often lead isolated lives. Sociopaths are notoriously lacking in empathy. On the contrary, someone who is empathetic is perceived as warm and caring. But are there exercises to develop empathy? Let's find out some!

Research shows that empathy and emotional intelligence are partly innate and partly learned. Everyone can improve, however. Here are eight ways to improve and develop your empathy!

Suggestions and exercises to develop empathy

1: The firs challenge

Take on challenging experiences that push you out of your comfort zone. Learn a new skill, for example, as a musical instrument, a hobby or a foreign language. Develops a new professional competence. Doing things like this will make you modest, and humility is a key factor for empathy.

2: Get out of your usual environment

Travel, especially towards new places and cultures. It gives you a new point of view and helps you appreciate others more.

3: Get feedback

Ask for feedback on your interpersonal skills (eg listening) from family, friends and colleagues. Then check back with them periodically to see how you are.

4: Explore the heart not just the head

Read literature that explores personal relationships and emotions. This has been shown to improve the empathy of young doctors.

5: Put yourself in others' shoes

Try to talk to others to understand what it means to "be in their place", to have their problems and concerns. Also try to understand how they perceived the experiences you both shared.

6: Review your prejudices

We all have hidden prejudices (and sometimes not so hidden) that interfere with our ability to listen and empathize. These are often focused on visible factors such as age, race and gender. Don't you think you have prejudices? Think again, we have them all!

7: Cultivate your curiosity

What can you learn from a very young colleague who is "inexperienced?" What can you learn from a client that you consider "dull"? Curious people ask many questions, which lead them to develop a stronger understanding of the people around them.

8: Ask better questions

Ask three or four thoughtful and even provocative questions to every conversation you have with clients or colleagues.

TRUST WHAT YOU DO AND SAY

Self-confidence conveys confidence in others. The opposite also happens: when someone is doubtful or insecure, he activates a defensive response from the listener. It is not difficult to be sure: one simply needs to give the person one is a chance; without forgetting that, inside the person you are, you also find what you want to be hidden.

Fear is one of the emotions that most of all could make communication tense and, therefore, in certain contexts an obstacle to interpersonal relationships. On many occasions, to get away from the flu, only a little training is needed. To do this, we try to prevent our communication from having dominance over breaks, looking for conversation rather than speech or monologue.

We don't need to become talkative people, very clever or funny. We simply need to find naturalness in communication. For example, an over-set discourse can be interpreted by the listener as an attempt to hide something, while the only thing we try to hide is that we are afraid to show ourselves as we are. Why?

It is our duty to try to highlight some aspects of our personality and work with it to make sure that everyone has more consideration for themselves. For this we will try to set some basic rules:

1. The goals I want to achieve must be established on our own initiative without being influenced by others. If this were not the case, confidence in ourselves would diminish, given that

we will underestimate our potential by never reaching the finish line.

2. All my goals will be able to satisfy my person only in the event that he will fully respond to my values.

3. Increasing self-confidence is a consequence of the goals we have achieved.

4. As we can see everything revolves around our true essence, the only thing that can make us believe in ourselves.

With the term self-esteem we want to highlight an essential element, which would mean: evaluate. First of all, in fact, one must be aware of two things: do we have problems increasing our self-esteem or evaluating ourselves?

These discomforts come from profound origins which, according to some in-depth studies on the subject, are due to the adolescent age of the person concerned. Precisely for this reason, people ask for advice in this regard, preferring more exercises to improve self-esteem than a real specialist in the field.

Making mistakes is a condition that unites a lot of individuals and does not involve having a low self-confidence. This can be seen as an incentive to have to do more and more!

Can decisions be included in self-esteem exercises?

Decisions allow you to build your own life paths. And for this nobody has to think that a person is not able to make a decision: unconsciously we live our life making decisions and making choices.

But why do we sometimes feel stuck? Simple, for fear of making mistakes. Who doesn't make mistakes? We must let that weight slip away and keep our minds quiet so we don't lose control.

In some cases instead we let ourselves go in search of the "best" solution to try not to harm our feelings and those of others. To make our self-esteem crumble may have depended on our mania to control everything and everyone so when something goes beyond this, how do we feel? Perhaps lost.

And this is precisely what must not happen.

Self-Esteem Exercises - Keep Your Mood Balanced

According to some research it has been found that changing one's mood is not impossible. In fact it can be associated without problems with the consideration that everyone has of himself. This is why the more you are in a good mood the more positive thoughts are strong.

To balance one's energy one must be calm and not be stressed before going to sleep because the bad mood causes discomfort and exhaustion. Then to download this tension it would be advisable to practice healthy sport.

The movement is needed to be able to keep one's energy level constant so that this method turns out to be better than eating chocolate. Tranquility and nature are very efficient natural cures.

Everyone knows their own person and knows how to evaluate when their energies reach high levels. For this reason it would be appropriate to carry out the most strenuous commitments in those specific moments! How does our mood change?

We value all the things that keep us calm and we try never to miss them! For example, music can relax all the muscles of our body (of course I mean relaxing music like soul and not rock and roll!).

To be decisive for the mood is undoubtedly sleep: some people, if they do not sleep, are surly and suspicious. If we recognize ourselves in this it would be appropriate to rest.

9 exercises to increase self-esteem

Learning: the consideration one has of oneself is equal to our level of learning. Everything we have faced has unconsciously led us to set goals. For example, for an exam or whatever we have always been committed to bringing the level of self-esteem to increase and consequently to succeed in that particular field. In itself, our entire existence is based on continuous challenges, so it's enough just to be able to learn the right training.

Mind: this is where all our thoughts, negative or positive, are concentrated. Analyzing the negative ones it can be said that these can discourage the person bringing it to associate to its image sentences like "I'm not up to it", "I can't do it", "I'm not able" so as to escape from what one has more fear. All we will have to do will be to disguise these thoughts in a positive light "here is another problem, I have already faced it and I will manage to solve it again".

Improve your aesthetic appearance: it will seem almost banal, but devoting a few minutes to taking care of your body is good for self-esteem. If we feel beautiful, others will also be able to appreciate us for what we are.

Physical activity: our body must keep fit and in good shape. A good purpose would be to start playing sports with the arrival of the new year!

Finding one's inner being: according to a Chinese elder, the most effective weapon to defeat battles is to know oneself. The best thing to do would be to write down what happens to us in a diary, sometimes there will be positive and some negative experiences. This will allow us to bring out our true essence by becoming invincible.

Helping a needy person: helping a person in need, even if we don't know it, allows us to feel good and have a greater self-esteem.

Speaking slowly: all the most powerful men speak in a clear and slow way to make people understand their own authority. What does it cost us to try? I recommend not to overdo it.

Saying "No": in life you have to say some no otherwise everyone will make fun of our person. For example in a work environment he will be able to show us strength and tenacity.

Choose your goal to pursue: we try to set goals, small, and then succeed in achieving them. This will make us believe in ourselves and consequently get very high.

ALWAYS SMILE

To say that a smile opens many doors may seem like a phrase made, a common place. Not for this reason it is to be considered false. The smile breaks down barriers, builds an emotional climate of affection and helps to alleviate tensions. Among other things, it's free.

To motivate ourselves, we think that a smile is a sign of peace and acceptance: an affectionate gesture that represents the best recipe for good communication. A gesture that breaks the ice and invites confidence. Nothing better to improve interpersonal relationships than to start every new meeting with a smile. Several studies have shown that people have a lot more confidence in approaching someone who smiles rather than someone who doesn't.

GOOD MANNERS

Good manners will never go out of style or stop being the keys that open the most important doors. Furthermore, with practice, one gains naturalness, ceasing to transmit the feeling of artificiality that many interpret as falsehood, rather than as respect and consideration.

Obviously, there are many courtesy rules that are only ceremonial. Others, on the other hand, are fundamental and should not be lost. For example, the good habit of saying goodbye and taking leave, thanking others, not interrupting others when they talk, letting others pass first ... Small gestures that show that you are willing to tune into others.

In this regard, it is appropriate to underline the importance of a good habit that is now lost and that has to do with the mobile phone. Unless you are waiting for an urgent call, the best thing to do is to leave your cell phone away from our field of action and sight so that it cannot distract us. We certainly won't lose anything important if we leave the phone aside for a while. Indeed, we could only benefit from it.

LEARN TO MANAGE ANGER

Managing anger, like all other emotions, is another habit you learn. There is a golden rule that can help us in moments of great anger: we only have to do three things, that is to say nothing, do nothing and remain calm. That's all. The wrath certainly won't make conflict resolution easier.

As in other cases, it's just a matter of training. This attitude is acquired through repetition. We just have to wait for a part of the energy that leads to this emotion to dissipate, enough to convey the message in the best way for us and for the relationship. Similarly, we will send a message of self-control and show respect for ourselves and others.

Interpersonal relationships can deteriorate, in most cases due to bad management of anger. When this emotion takes control over us, we show our worst side, coming to be very cruel especially with the people we love, because they are also the people whose weaknesses we know best.

I am sure that you will certainly have experienced powerful emotions, capable of affecting you negatively: today we will discover how to manage anger.

Anger is an emotion that is sometimes so disruptive that it is capable of making you combine some trouble.

Let's find out how to deal with anger!

Has anyone in anger committed some reckless action, or ruined a relationship, or had to pay that explosion at a high price?

We lose control, convinced that we are right and we stamp our feet to be recognized.

We make huge messes when we let ourselves be overwhelmed by this emotion.

We get angry because we don't feel sufficiently considered, due to the spirit of competition, to defend ourselves or defend someone who is dear to us from someone else.

When we think that a person is responsible for causing us damage.

We get more angry with the people we love, because we expect them to be understood, we expect them to respect our values, our rules.

When we don't find someone to get angry with, we get angry with ourselves, for having done something wrong, not having understood, being put in complicated situations ...

We assume a contracted posture, muscular tension, the blood is directed towards legs and arms (this is why from anger we have greater strength), the heartbeat increases and we are like prehistoric men ready to fight.

But what is anger?

Anger is an emotion that we manifest from an early age. It is a primordial emotion determined by the instinct to defend oneself and survive the environment one lives.

We tend to think that anger is the wrong thing. It is an emotion and therefore has its usefulness and needs to be lived. Meanwhile, remember that he is telling you something important: your values have been violated. It is useful because it is the tool that makes you understand that the limit of "tolerance" that we give to others and to ourselves has been exceeded.

That's what we do with that anger, what we have to work on.

If we turn it into violent aggression towards others, then it becomes an instrument of destruction. But think if that energy was channeled constructively. The best thing would be to learn to handle that anger, which comes and thanks that comes because it is telling you important things.

These three exercises could help you.

LET IT GO

When the anger comes, let it flow without putting a stopper. If you block it in, sooner or later it will blow you up, just like the water does when you try to block it, sooner or later you will find a way to flow outside. Find a place where you can vent if there is need: go by car, secluded and let off steam. Sing, scream, cry, beat your fists, do what you feel like doing. Another idea if you can go in the middle of nature, in a secluded place and scream all your anger, touching the earth, a tree. Connect with the energy of nature and download your anger there, nature will be happy to receive your energy to transform it

WATCH THE SITUATION FROM THE OUTSIDE

An exercise I do is to see the situation from above. Imagine seeing the dynamics that triggered the anger that takes place below us, where there are all but the protagonists, including you, and looking at the scene as if you were an emotionally uninvolved observer. Then I ask to observe the scene in the shoes of the other / others that are part of the scene itself. In most cases, with this dissociation, one realizes that the other one you below is taking too much and that situation can be managed differently, reducing anger.

TIME LINE

What does it mean? Put on the timeline. Look at that situation that is generating anger in a temporal perspective and ask yourself if in a week it will still be so important, in a month, in a year, in 5 years. What meaning will that situation seen on the timeline have? Does it have the same value? And if even in a week this anger will be reduced, can you immediately reconsider the situation and adopt a more rational method?

DETAILS ARE IMPORTANT

There are some attitudes, or small details, that significantly increase the quality of interpersonal relationships. These are simple gestures that speak of nobility and good disposition towards others. Incorporating them into our natural way of being is a great idea. Among these gestures we find:

1. Making sincere praise: usually we do not have the habit of sharing our positive thoughts about others, but doing so is always a great source of satisfaction;
2. Call people by name;
3. Let the importance of a problem be established by the person who is experiencing it;
4. In a controversy, indicate to the other that we value his point of view and that we want to understand it;
5. Show interest in what the other feels;
6. Don't try to change the way people think.

Good interpersonal relationships are the result of effort. Although some people come into the world with a greater predisposition towards easy interaction with others, we all have to learn. This is especially true when we have had a long history marked by the difficulty in sharing the long list of conflicts we are experiencing.

If we can improve the quality of our interpersonal relationships, all aspects of our life will benefit them. This in turn will increase self-confidence and a sense of general well-being. When our interactions with others are constructive, we feel more motivated and happier.

THE STRATEGIC DIALOGUE

If we look back at the situations we experience every day, we will find that our reactions to the same circumstances have changed over time.

At work, perhaps, meetings that once frightened us now are no longer a problem; during dinners with friends, instead, if a few years ago the presence of strangers intimidated us, now we consider it a happy opportunity to meet people with whom to share our passions.

Certainly, as we grow up, we gain experience and mature, but this development is not taken for granted: the ability to work on oneself and continuously improve oneself must also be acquired and stimulated. In this way our actions and reactions to events will become more effective every day and will help us to be better and better, both with ourselves and with others.

To achieve this very important goal for our wellbeing, we can intervene on several fronts, including the language we use on a daily basis.

The words with which people describe, interpret and elaborate situations allow them to face them with greater or lesser success: this is why, if we think of some events that have changed us, we will realize that today we not only see them with different eyes but, in the talk about it, we also use words, expressions and a completely new tone of voice.

Not everyone is aware of how much language can determine both our interpersonal relationships and that of ourselves, as well as the way we manage everyday life.

Not everyone knows that the persuasive language is the most powerful tool to overcome conflicts and create harmony, going to act both on our mind and on our emotions.

This type of communication stimulates empathy, mutual understanding, confrontation and, consequently, our personal growth. All this is possible because persuasion does not only make use of the indicative language, with instructions, information and explanations, but also of the performative language, evoking sensations capable of changing the ways in which we interpret the world.

The main verbal communication strategies used in the Strategic Dialogue are 3:

1. To join, that is to use a language that exhorts the other to make experiences that can change his opinion, his point of view. It is not a matter of impositions or orders, but of a suggestive and persuasive communication, which evokes in people the feeling of being able to do something completely different from what they are used to, overcoming their limits.

2. To evoke, that is, to use a language that, through analogies and images, helps to project oneself into concrete situations. There is no need to think of anything too complex: even the very simple phrase "I slept like a child" fulfills this technique of Strategic Dialogue, with an image that evokes a clear experience in the listener.

3. Restructure, that is, change the structure and sequence of words used by a person to offer them different points of view without changing the content of his speech, in an indirect way. To restructure you can use paraphrases, strategic questions that guide the interlocutor in a certain direction, narratives, suggestive aphorisms.

Persuasively communicating means the right thing at the right time, being able to win the interest of the listener, without boring him or bothering him with distracting attitudes, keeping the attention on the topic to be treated and instilling confidence in what we are saying.

Taking into account the fact that most of the public is mistrustful by nature and many are not even interested, it must be conquered as a terrain on a battlefield.

Persuasive communication is the main ingredient of personal and professional success, an expressive modality that blends together logic, organizational capacity, problem solving, empowerment, deduction skills, assertiveness, sensitivity and empathy.

Being persuasive, convincing people about their ideas and projects is definitely a gift, but a lot can be done to improve. Psychological research has revealed several effective techniques, which we summarize below. In presenting an argument, the contradictions present in one's own discourse must be highlighted, that is, different points of view must be presented, and then one decidedly chosen, to the detriment of the others. This makes what is becoming more credible, because it is as if one were not afraid to confront the ideas opposed to one's own.

Show the different aspects of a problem: a topic expressed with intellectual honesty, balanced, which takes into consideration the different perspectives is therefore certainly more convincing, and makes no difference if these contrary arguments are tackled at the beginning, at the end or in the middle of the speech: the important thing is to explain why they are rejected.

Show conviction. Research shows that humans prefer boldness to competence. Even the most skeptical people tend to be at least partly persuaded by a speaker who shows he believes in what he says.

Show enthusiasm. Enthusiasm is an emotion that can be transmitted. So letting yourself be pervaded by this emotion while talking is a must. Always start with statements or premises that will surely be accepted by the public. This builds the basis for preparing people for acceptance of subsequent points of view.

Speech speed: speak quickly if it is assumed that the public does not agree with what is stated (do not allow time to reflect properly); speak slowly if you are sure to expose topics that can receive public approval (the reflection confirms the data presented by the speaker). If the public has a neutral position, speak quickly enough (it can be useful not to bore him). To be more convincing it is necessary to show emotions, even leaving one's professionalism aside.

Show anger or frustration because things are not going as you would like can convince your audience more than many words. Reach positive conclusions. Between "you will stop making so many mistakes" or "you will be much more precise", choose the second one. Same thing between: "you will stop feeling so tired" or "you will feel much more energetic." Positive statements tend to be more persuasive. What needs to be done is to get the public to dream of something better. Instead of telling people what they can avoid, leading them to rethink their problems.

THE PRESENTATION

Our most important business card is the presentation, how we place ourselves with others and what we communicate before we even talk and make suggestions.

The impression must be excellent, unexceptionable, excellent, it goes without saying that it must be adapted to every environment that we have to face, because the place tells much more than people and even before them.

If the place is formal we must adapt, trying to be elegant but not excessive, we must not give the impression of having put on the only ceremonial dress that we possess, maybe even out of fashion, elegance is not made of excesses but of simplicity and good taste and does not even require an excessive expense.

Furthermore we must not forget that adapting to the environment so as not to be out of tune with it is as important as not selling off what we are not, we will give a false representation of ourselves that would be discovered within a few minutes, and therefore we will no longer be credible whatsoever truth we are willing to tell.

The advice that always works is to mediate in the middle way, pointing out our characteristics but not forgetting what the others, those who are already in the environment and are well adapted to them, must be respected as well as their rules of behavior and management of the public or staff.

Obviously without losing sight of the purpose that is to conquer work or the market and therefore it is necessary to play cunning without being false or lying.

The presentation with a good handshake, sure, is a great way to give a good impression already, remember that there is no need to crush that of the other to look stronger, it would only bother you, and if it is a determined but delicate woman.

Women often wear rings in the hand to be tightened, pay attention to them and make them present to the person you have not tightened too much so that the part in contact with the ring is not hurt, the lady will appreciate the gesture twice, both for the courtesy and for the fact of having noticed one of its accessories.

Let's take a practical example.

If it is a job interview it is necessary to present yourself professionally in the right way, but we must also be sure that it is the right job for us, so we must have a knowledge of ourselves, of our desires and expectations that allow us to make the choice just not to find oneself repented and disappointed by a job that will become heavier, boring and certainly not gratifying, with the consequence of suffering stress, low self-esteem and evaluation of our abilities and potential that could not be better invested.

TRUST IN YOURSELF AND PRACTICE YOGA

If it is a job interview it is necessary to present yourself professionally in the right way, but we must also be sure that it is the right job for us, so we must have a knowledge of ourselves, of our desires and expectations that allow us to make the choice just not to find oneself repented and disappointed by a job that will become heavier, boring and certainly not gratifying, with the consequence of suffering stress, low self-esteem and evaluation of our abilities and potential that could not be better invested.

Psychology, in general, asserts that the lack of self-esteem derives from a difference that develops between what one would like to be and what one really is.

When there is a lot of discrepancy between the two visions, there is low self-esteem and value.

The causes of the lack of self-confidence must be sought, as we have previously mentioned, in childhood and adolescence, in the way in which emotions and relationships with others have been considered and managed. However, whatever the cause of your lack of trust in you, it is useless now to blame the parents or anyone who has played a role in this. Surely they did all this unconsciously and also with the best intentions.

But yoga teaches us that the past cannot be changed and the future is unreal. Therefore, we can only act in the present and it is what really matters. Moreover, from a more spiritual point of view, we know that every soul chooses the family in which to be born and grow because, it is through the relationship with this that it discovers itself.

"Trust in your distrust", because it is through the observation of yourself and the acceptance of what you define your weaknesses, that you can make a leap of awareness and grow as a person.

Yoga in general increases the awareness of yourself, putting you in touch with your true self. The more you are in touch with the true Self, the more you flow into life and trust yourself and everything around you.

As explained in the previous paragraph, low self-esteem develops when what you would like to be is different from what you are in the present.

All this is caused by imagination, which takes over and must therefore be fought.

Yoga allows you to live more and more the present moment, the here and now, and so all the ghosts of the mind, as in this case the imagination that causes little trust, slowly disappear to make room only for what is real .

Furthermore the practice of asanas, thanks to the strengthening of will power and the development of patience, allows you to face your difficulties day by day and slowly overcome them. This over time gives rise to an incredible trust in yourself, not only in practice but also in life.

The yoga positions that develop self-confidence are mostly those of balance on their feet and those that strengthen the lower limbs.

This is because it is in the strength of concentration, of inner balance and of "walking on one's own legs" that one's inner strength develops.

These positions stimulate Muladhara chakra, the first chakra, and therefore also the earth element, increasing rooting and self-confidence.

The lack of self-esteem is a symptom of an inner weakness, lack of concentration and balance.

The Pran mudra, which I am going to illustrate to you, can help you activate the root chakra by increasing vitality, reducing physical and mental fatigue, increasing the ability to resist facing obstacles and thus increasing self-confidence.

Use this mudra when you feel you need it, for about 10 minutes a day, and keep practicing it for a short time or anyway until you feel better about this aspect of your life.

Practicing this gesture is very simple:

- Take a meditative position;
- Put your hands on your knees and join the tip of your little finger, ring finger and thumb;
- Breathe consciously and image of being a strong tree with deep roots.

You can also mentally repeat this sankalpa: "I am strong and rooted like a tree that remains impassive to the elements, so I face the challenges of life with commitment and serenity".

If you practice yoga and meditation consistently, I am sure that the little achievements in practice will help you incredibly in life. You will be stronger both mentally and physically, you will be able to better control your thoughts and over time your low self-esteem will give way to greater self-confidence.

CONCLUSIONS

Who has not thought at least once in his life: "Ah! If I had said that thing at the right time".Indeed, shyness, as well as insecurity, can sometimes make even the simplest actions difficult.

What is shyness? Shyness is a particular "personality trait" of an individual who always makes him feel out of place and out of time, makes him remain silent and does not let him express his opinion for fear of making mistakes and being judged by others, that the it only turns red if someone looks at him, and so on. This leads to profound insecurity when it comes to dealing with a person or situation and you understand that it may not be a good experience. The good news is that nobody is born shy! In fact, there are only three instinctive fears that each of us has from birth: the fear of falling, the fear of loud noises and the fear of being abandoned.

We know this because when a newborn hears a loud noise it starts and cries. Or when he has the feeling of losing support beneath him, or even when he is deprived of his parents' physical contact for a long time, his instinctive reaction is to cry. Beyond these, all other types of fear are acquired, or rather learned, throughout life. Many of these fears are taught to us (with all the best intentions) by parents, the school, the media or certain experiences we make.

<u>We must imagine our brain that at birth is like a new notebook with all the blank pages.</u>

As soon as we come into the world, the people around us begin to compete to write in that notebook. Some write useful things to us, others write deleterious instructions such as the mechanism of shyness, the fear of others' judgment, low self-esteem and so on. It is of fundamental importance, however, to understand that like all things written in a notebook can be erased and corrected or replaced with more useful ones, so it is possible to change the conviction of being shy.

What are the tips for overcoming shyness?

Never call yourself "shy": How many times have you heard yourself say, "How shy you are!" or you thought it yourself. If it has happened to you a few times in your life to be shy, insecure or embarrassed, do not call yourself either shy or insecure or embarrassed.

Change your internal dialogue, start telling yourself "Ok, that time I was shy but in many other situations I got off really brilliantly."

Clear the definitions: you are always different and if you have behaved like a shy person, you are not necessarily so in all circumstances. Don't let yourself be conditioned by prejudices and throw away that too rigid meter with which you judge yourself, in search of a perfection that does not exist and that nobody possesses.

Learn from your mistakes: Remember that any wrong action you take cannot be corrected, you cannot jump back in time to change what has happened, but you can make yourself aware of the mistake you made and work to stop committing it. For every mistake you make, you automatically give yourself a chance, stick to a challenge: that of not being able to commit it anymore. You must win it.

Resume control of the situation: If you happen to feel redness or overheating, agitation and sweating, take back the reins of the situation! Take slow deep breaths and let fresh air in your lungs, you will refresh yourself, you will supply more oxygen to your brain to become shiny again and you will regain your usual color.

In all probability, you generally know those situations where all this occurs: don't give us more weight than we should, but simply give them the importance they deserve. To have a valid and consistent yardstick to measure the emotional burden that these situations should determine in you, take a look at how others around you behave: are they at ease? And what prevents you from being? Act at the root of the matter, understand that in reality you have nothing to fear and face (or rather, live) the situation with the serenity you deserve.

To believe in yourself you need to be aware of the qualities and results you have achieved. Stop looking only at those who are better than you, look also at your position and say: "Yes, it is true that I can improve and aspire to be like that very confident person that I admire, but it is also true that "it's a nice line of people behind me". We often envy those who are better than us in a certain field and we do not realize how foolish and limiting this is: there is always someone better than us in a given field, the point is that we do not keep in mind those peculiarities of life in which we we are better than others.

At this point, I hope you found the answers you were looking for. Put these tips into practice, be constant, get used to thinking of you in this new light, you'll see that with the right training you can definitely defeat the senseless shyness and insecurity you feel today.

You know very well that it is not an easy or even a short process. Start like this, trust yourself, and you will be able to complete this new path.

I propose a simple game. Think of the word "fear": how many synonyms do you know? Which come to mind instantly? You will probably think of terms like anxiety, fear, terror, anxiety, fear, fear, panic, dismay, trembling. Now think of the word "courage". Can you immediately indicate synonyms? In all probability, you would need a little more time. And then to think of terms like temerity, boldness, daring.

What can we deduce from this little experiment?
Basically two things:

The first is that we know different synonyms of "fear", a higher number than we know of the word "courage". Probably, in our life we have become much more familiar with fear than with courage, so much so that we have different modalities and nuances available to define and name it.

The second is that the synonyms of "fear" are part of our everyday language, while the synonyms of "courage" appear to us outdated, belonging to distant eras, certainly not exactly current. Hardness and recklessness are characteristics of condottieri, heroes and leaders of the past. Or at least we usually attribute these qualities to the great characters that history has handed down to us.

And yet, the uncertain and liquid era that we are living in is clamoring for the need to exercise courage. Courage is needed in small or large everyday choices, in the professional as well as in private life.

To overcome shyness and "social phobia" there are several

techniques and tricks you could follow. Primarily, it is about acting on your self-confidence and your way of experiencing relationships with each other.

One of the things that makes overcoming being shy is that these people tend to think that it is a problem that only a few others experience.

This makes them capable of thinking that there is something wrong with them, destroying their already fragile self-esteem even more.

In reality, as we have mentioned, there are many people who live at least in a situation of shyness during their lives. Many public figures such as actors, singers and politicians are also shy, but have learned to manage the phenomenon successfully.

Realizing that shyness is common and, more importantly, commonly overcome, the problem starts to seem much less debilitating.

In the digital age in which we live, the best therapy to overcome shyness is to practice speaking with family and friends, perhaps through short videos.

Appearing on video, writing a blog, publishing your thoughts will help you understand how to overcome shyness by having an attitude of openness to the world. Do this exercise consistently and try to improve yourself more every day.

Remember that social skills, like all skills, are highly perishable. You can't expect to master them if you don't practice them daily. So don't wait to test your social skills in situations where the outcome is important to you. Rather, practice as much as possible in situations of little relevance or where you feel safe.

Continue to practice in everyday situations, for example, with the supermarket assistant or the waiter of your favorite restaurant.

The common approach that timid people put in place to overcome anxiety is to immediately undergo a great social challenge, often without success.

In fact, the problem with this strategy is that if you can't socialize without problems, you simply reinforce the idea that you already have in your head of being shy and clumsy, that you can't change, that socializing is threatening and that the only way to to get rid of those threatening feelings is to avoid any kind of opening.

Success generates success when shyness is overcome: the more successful you are, the more confident you will become in yourself.

Instead of setting big goals, it aims at small goals that seem less threatening. First of all, simply learn to work on eye contact with people. When, for example, you ask your colleague a question for work, look him in the eye while he answers you.

Try to generate interactions with people you know and have already had contacts with. For example, when you have coffee in the morning at the bar, ask your bartender how his day goes. If you need help finding something in a store, ask a clerk to help you.

Treat your everyday small social interactions like little experiments and take advantage of every opportunity to get out of your "comfort zone" and create a dialogue.

If your main question is how to overcome shyness, you should know that one of the reasons people worry about social gatherings is that they are unsure of what they should say or how they should act in certain situations.

Uncertainty is the true primary source of anxiety. According to some research, people forget their anxiety more easily if they are involved in activities that are useful to others and give them a predetermined role or job.

For example, many people who call themselves shy have no problem talking to strangers if they are part of their job. If you are trying to overcome your shyness to make new friends, consider dedicating your time to organizations that align with your interests and values. Taking an example, if you like politics, dedicate yourself to an activity as a volunteer. If you are very religious, attend the group in your parish.

Shyness is therefore a psychological condition on which it is possible to work to better face life and the relationship with others. This can be done, in the long run, by doing a work on ourselves, first of all by improving self-esteem and following simple tips to experience everyday life with greater serenity and security.

Everything I write is pure theory until you put it into practice in your everyday life.

And so you came to the end. What do you think about what you read? I am very curious to know your opinion and I would also like to know if you think my content is useful for your personal growth path. If so, then please leave a positive review on the Amazon website.

Made in the USA
Middletown, DE
17 July 2020

13054800R00066